The Good Housekeeping
CHILDREN'S PARTY BOOK

The Good Housekeeping
CHILDREN'S PARTY BOOK

By MARY BREEN

Favours by VERNA BREEN
Edited by HUGH W. EWING

Illustrated by
HAMILTON GREENE and NORA S. UNWIN

The National Magazine Company, London

First Published in England 1946

Made and Printed in Great Britain by
Hazell, Watson & Viney, Ltd., London and Aylesbury

Foreword

THIS book offers you a collection of parties, planned from invitation to good-bye. Most of them are centred round a definite theme, because a child's imagination is rich in make-believe, and he loves the just-pretend play of being a pirate, an engine-driver, or a circus clown.

A child needs these occasional parties with their colour, surprises, and gaiety. Even though he spends all his waking hours playing, his day-to-day games do not take the place of parties, with their ceremony and exciting novelty. Furthermore, parties acquaint the child with the ways of being a gracious host and a charming guest.

You may find some of these parties too elaborate. You may like the games in one, the decorations in another. Shift them round in any way you please; or choose your own theme and select games for your party from the special chapters on games.

But do have parties for your children—birthday parties and holiday ones. Unless the party is to be a complete surprise, let the child help you with the preparations. Sharing in the work will give him a sense of responsibility and develop his resourcefulness. More than that, the fun of doing things together cements the family ties of understanding and love.

Contents

PART I

PARTIES FOR THE THREE TO TEN YEAR OLDS

CHAPTER   PAGE

1. *HINTS ON PARTY PLANNING* . . 11

   How to plan parties that are fun to give and to attend.

2. *A PARTY FOR A THREE-YEAR-OLD* . 18

   Peter has his first party with his friends.

3. *ROSEMARY'S FOURTH BIRTHDAY* . 20

   Unexpected things happen when fourteen children get together.

4. *AN A B C PARTY* 23

   For boys and girls who are just learning their letters.

5. *A MODEL RAILWAY PARTY* . . 29

   Young engineers bring their own rails and trains and build a main-line railway.

6. *A DOLL PARTY* 33

   Favourite dolls are the honoured guests.

7. *A HALLOWE'EN PARTY* . . . 40

   Children of four, five and six years make their acquaintance with Hallowe'en fun.

8. *RAINY DAY DRESS-UP* . . . 46

   One of those wonderful parties that just happen. For boys and girls up to ten years.

CHAPTER   PAGE

9. *A CHRISTMAS PARTY* 48
   A merry Christmas celebration for children from four
   to ten years.

10. *AN EASTER BIRTHDAY PARTY* . . 52
    The traditional games in both indoor and outdoor
    settings.

11. *SOAP BUBBLE PARTY* 60
    An ever-popular pastime becomes a party for boys and
    girls.

12. *PETER PAN PICNIC* 64
    Even Captain Hook puts in his appearance at this out-
    door frolic for children from seven to ten.

13. *MAKE UP YOUR OWN PARTIES* . . 70
    Some additional ideas from which to choose if you
    wish to plan a party for yourself.

14. *MORE GAMES FOR PARTIES AND PICNICS* 77

PART II

JOLLY PARTIES FOR THE EARLY 'TEENS

15. *A HALLOWE'EN PARTY FOR OLDER
    CHILDREN* 92
    The Hallowe'en witch joins in the revels.

16. *A FAMILY CHRISTMAS PARTY* . . 98
    Some ways of contributing to this traditional feast of
    plenty.

17. *A GOOD NEIGHBOURS' PARTY FOR
    CHRISTMAS EVE* 105
    The spirit of Yuletide sharing inspires this party.

CHAPTER   PAGE

18. *"GREAT AMBITION" PARTY*   .   .   110
A chance to be what you want to be makes this a novel
and amusing party.

19. *A BOY'S BIRTHDAY PARTY*   .   .   117
With the rougher kind of games boys like to play with
boys.

20. *TREASURE HUNT PARTY*   .   .   .   124
Amateur detectives outdo Scotland Yard in running
down clues.

21. *A VALENTINE PARTY, MODERN STYLE*   126
A fast-tempo party replaces the lavender-and-lace
affair of long ago.

22. *CIRCUS PARTY*   135
Fun under the "big top," indoors and out.

23. *CAPTURE-THE-FLAG PARTY*   .   .   144
A lively open-air party for scout and club outings.

24. *GAMES FOR PICNICS AND OUT OF
DOORS*   146

25. *MORE INDOOR GAMES*   .   .   .   149

HINTS ON QUANTITIES   .   .   .   155

SOME SIMPLE PARTY DISHES   .   .   156

CLASSIFIED INDEX OF GAMES   .   .   158

PART I

PARTIES FOR THE
THREE TO TEN YEAR OLDS

HINTS ON

1

PARTY PLANNING

Many mothers are in a state of panic when the time comes for the first party for their first child. "How long should the party be?" "Who should be invited?" "What games will the children enjoy?" Their anxiety is easy to understand. Most of us cannot remember what we thought or liked when we were three or four, and the child who is having the party cannot be expected to set himself up as expert.

Some of us, however, are fortunate enough to have had experience with many children and many games, and to have learned from them the Do's and Don'ts of successful parties. In this chapter we are glad to share these tips with mothers and others who are interested in making their children's parties happy and long-remembered occasions.

The First Party

On his birthday the tiny child is king for a day. This is the one time during the year when his family and his friends—who are the entire universe to a three- or four-year-old—acknowledge his sway and pay him homage. It is inconceivable to him that anyone else should claim a share in it. When I made the mistake of telling Nicky that his birthday was mine too, he looked completely disgusted at my attempt to cut into his glory, and said, "It is not *your birthday*. It's mine. It can't be yours."

Let the child have his day of days, then, and surround it with all the trappings of a real celebration. If he is only one or two, a simple iced cake with a sparkling candle and a new toy in bright wrappings are all that he needs to assure him that there is something very special about the day, and that whatever the fuss is all about, he has a very pleasant place right in the middle of it.

When he is three, or four, or five, he can have a real party. It may be a very small one with two or three of his playmates, or a really special one with extra guests. It may be simple or lavish. Whether it costs 5s. or £5, the party must be fun and the birthday child and his guests must have a happy time.

How Many Parties?

In addition to his own party, the child of three or four or five may be invited to celebrate the birthdays of other children of his own age. If the circle of family friends is large, it may be necessary to limit the number of invitations accepted for him. Some children take parties calmly in their stride. Others become over-stimulated and excited. The mother must decide for herself when her child is ready for group parties, and how many he can attend without too much emotional disturbance. As a general rule, children of this age should not attend more than six or eight a year.

Children of school age may receive even more invitations as the number of their acquaintances increases. Here, too, the child's own ability to cope with social situations is the best guide as to the number of parties that are wise for him.

Guard against over-strain, at holiday times especially. Children should celebrate Christmas and Easter with their friends, but too many parties are as indigestible as too many sweets.

WHO SHOULD BE INVITED?

The child's friends, is the best answer. Sometimes it is necessary to include favourite cousins and the children of his father's business associates. As far as possible, limit the guests to the boys and girls whom the little host regards as real friends. If the party is not to be a complete surprise, let him decide who should be invited, though his choice may, of course, have to be guided.

Children of three should have not more than four or five friends to their parties. Children of four may have an extra two or three. Ten or twelve guests are enough for a party for a five-year-old. Twenty is the maximum for children from six to ten. When these numbers must be exceeded, plan a general entertainment—a home-cinema, marionettes, or conjurer—rather than a programme of active games.

In searching for entertainers, make inquiries at your local high school or agent. Many of them have young hobbyists who would be glad to put on a show for a small charge, or even for the experience of performing before an audience.

HOW AGE AFFECTS PARTY PLANNING

To a great extent, a child's age determines how he can get along with other children, and what games he can play. Children under five are little individualists. They like to be with other children, but they are not mature enough physically, mentally, or socially for group games. That is why in the parties suggested for this group there are so many *Hunts* and simplified games which do not require active inter-play between the children.

Children who attend nursery school are likely to learn the fundamental lessons of social co-operation earlier than children who play alone or with one or two other children. In choosing your programme, take your lead from the child's past experiences and do not attempt anything that is too different, or which requires him to exert himself in a way to which he is not accustomed.

Try to have all the children of the same age. One of the greatest difficulties of party planning is to devise a satisfactory programme for children of varying ages. If you can't avoid a wide disparity, choose the kind of activities in which children compete as individuals—Hunts, puzzle pictures, drawing, or make-something games; or, enlist the older boys and girls as assistants, and judges for team and group games. Puppet shows, films and conjurers are also good for such situations.

Playing the Games

Plan a complete programme which will fill every minute from the time the first guest arrives till the last one departs. Include a few extra games or attractions to fill any emergency. If you are shaky on the details, write your programme on a 3-in. by 5-in. card and attach it to your wrist with a rubber band. Most professional leaders do this when they are experimenting with new games.

The programme is your safety valve. Do not use it as a hard-and-fast formula. If the children suggest games of their own or new variations, let them play them by all means. Parties should be free and spontaneous, but when children get into their party clothes they are sometimes shy and constrained. They know that this fine living-room is not the place for the "wild and woolly" games they play in the garden, and they are at a loss to know what to do next. Unless something is offered to them, sheer boredom or discomfort often forces them to revert to the noisy, outdoor games they know best.

Explain games clearly. Wait quietly for attention before explaining the rules. Go through the game once, if necessary, to be sure that the procedure is understood by everyone. Change the game while interest is still high. Introduce a note of adventure or make-believe. The Magic Trail game can be made a search for pirate treasure, by giving the pirates red bandanas to wear on their heads, and a telescope through which to follow their string trail.

If any of the children do not want to participate, try to find something else that will entertain them. Do not force them to take part. Frequently a young child will go off and play with a train or look at a picture book and ignore the other children. Such a child is probably not ready for group play, and pressure will not hurry the process.

Older children who threaten to become bumptious can usually be made completely co-operative by singling them out for a conspicuous part in a game, or by giving them some specific responsibility.

If the party is to celebrate a birthday, allow fifteen or twenty minutes for opening the presents and playing with them. Wrappings will fly, if the children are under seven. Anticipate this, and have a waste-paper basket handy to collect the debris when you are ready to start the games.

Plan a quiet game before tea. After the meal, have a guessing game, or some similar game, so that children who are called for can leave without disrupting the group; or tell a story, or sing songs. The last is the best of all possible choices.

At what Time should the Party be held?

Most parents agree that parties should be held at the time which most easily fits into the children's daily routine. For very young children, a morning party, followed by the simplest of dinners, is occasionally favoured. This has the advantage that after the meal the children are taken home for the afternoon nap. The usual time, however, is the afternoon, when games are followed by a simple tea.

Older children are sometimes allowed evening parties, which start with a supper; or the lightest possible refreshments may be served during the evening.

How long should the Party last?

Most parties for young children are planned for two hours. This is just half an hour too long for children under five or six, unless the party can be held outdoors. Unlike adults, children not only are seldom late in arriving, but often appear a half-hour ahead of time. Besides that, parents are frequently delayed in calling for them. When this happens, you have three hours to plan for instead of two.

Anticipate these possibilities by arranging the party from three-thirty to five o'clock, and then planning a programme which will take care of early arrivals and late stayers. Then you won't be faced with the dilemma in which Rosemary's mother found herself. (*Chapter 3.*)

Even for school children under ten, parties should never last longer than three hours, including the time for supper or refreshments.

Party Food

If you look for tempting new concoctions in the menus given in this book, you will probably be disappointed. The very good reason for their absence is that children do not have adventurous palates when away from home. They are hesitant about experimenting with new tastes and new dishes. Mothers can prepare the scene for introducing strange foods, but the hostess can hardly be expected to do this for eight or ten children.

Children appreciate and are delighted with novelty in their meals, but the unique touches should be confined to the way the food is arranged and served. A ball of ice cream may masquerade as a bunny head, but the child can see at a glance that the head is really ice cream.

The Party Table

The table is a high-spot at a party, and should look as gay and attractive as possible. Obviously this is not an occasion for your best linen and china, and if you must use a polished table, avoid heartbreaks by having it well protected with one of those gay, spongeable cloths now on the market, or with some bright cover whose fate won't cause you any anxiety. Accidents are bound to happen sometimes, and no child at a party should feel unduly embarrassed over them.

Prizes

There is considerable controversy about the wisdom of prize-giving. Some adults feel very strongly that too many prizes distort a child's sense of values. He no longer plays for fun, but for the booty he can gather.

Now, if a child is accustomed to receiving prizes at other parties, he will expect them at yours. If you have a strong conviction against giving them, thrash out the problem with the mothers of your children's friends; or make your point with the children when they are old enough to understand. One way of removing the onus is to give the prizes a purpose and meaning. Encourage the child who is having the party to help make them. Then the prizes will have a greater value than the pampering of acquisitive instincts.

If you do have prizes, try to manage the games so that all the children will receive awards. If this is not possible, have general prizes or favours, so that each boy or girl has something to take home.

Distribute the prizes after tea or supper. When they are handed out after each game, the awards are frequently mislaid or broken before the party ends. Then you may have to send home a tearful, rather than a bright-eyed and happy child. Pin tickets or slips of paper on the coats or dresses of prize winners as promissory notes that awards will be given later.

Prize-giving can be made a game in itself by having a Lucky Dip, a Fish Pond, or a Jack Horner Pie, and letting the winners of the various games take turns in delving into their contents.

Should Mothers attend?

It is always helpful to have the assistance of one or two adults. If too many mothers want to come, however, and their presence threatens to disrupt or to hamper the children's party, let them play Bridge or have their own games in another room. But don't encourage a large group of adults to stand round and watch the children as if the latter were performers in a three-ring circus.

Cloakroom Arrangements

Give someone entire charge of the arrival and departure ends of the party to ensure that the wraps, shoes, etc., of each little guest are carefully put together, and to help with the taking off and putting on of outdoor things. Otherwise there is sure to be confusion, delay, and perhaps a stray garment to be returned the next day.

Away-from-home Parties

Vary the birthday celebrations with an occasional party away from home—a trip to the zoo, to a museum, a day at a fair, or a party to see a children's play. Many mothers have found these *away-from-home* parties the answer to the problem of celebrating the birthdays of children over six, when the family lives in a flat, or in a small house which has very little garden space.

Let the child invite several of his very closest friends to share the excursion. The birthday feast can be served at home, before or after the trip; or as a very special treat, the children might be taken to a restaurant which specializes in meals for youngsters.

Here's to Happy Parties!

The Do's and Donts', as you can see, are not so complicated after all. Plan the party carefully, anticipate any possible snags; then relax and have a good time and your merry little gathering will be a joy to you and your little guests. Here's wishing you all the happiest of parties!

A
PARTY *for a*
Three-year-old

2

PETER is a tow-haired curly-head, as social and extroverted as a
master of ceremonies.   For a week before his third birthday he kept
repeating to everyone he saw, "I'm going to have my birthday."   That
meant to him a party with friends, and a birthday cake with candles.

His two previous birthdays had been celebrated in lonely grandeur.
But now that he was almost three years old he wanted his birthday to
be a state occasion, and to have children of his own age to share in the
festivities.

The party was planned for three-thirty on a Saturday afternoon.
While Peter was having his nap, his mother set the party table, and hid
round the house an assortment of large, coloured wooden beads.   They
were placed in groups of two or three on tables, chairs, and in corners
where they would not be too hard to find.

Four boys and girls with whom Peter had played when he went to
the park were invited guests.   Promptly at three-twenty the first arrived,
scrubbed and shining and filled with excitement.   Under his arm he
carried a beautifully wrapped parcel.   The moment he saw Peter he
shoved the package at his tiny host and shouted, "Here's your present.
It's a boat.   Let's play with it."   No subtlety or indirection for this

young man. Paper flew in all directions. The boat was taken from its wrappings and the party had begun.

By a quarter to four all the children had arrived, accompanied by their mothers. Other presents were unwrapped and experimented with. Peter's toys were inspected, and then the children were ready for the hunting game.

Each child was given a paper bag in which to put the beads he found. After the last one was unearthed, the children sat on the floor, and were provided with shoe laces with which to string the beads. When the last one was completed and donned by its maker, Peter's mother played children's records on the gramophone. To some of them the children sang. To others they just listened with rapt attention. The last selection was a marching song to which the children pranced to the table.

There the birthday cake, standing proudly with its three red candles in the centre of the table, claimed their immediate interest. It was rather a special cake. Round its edge, small chocolate animals were set in the snowy icing, and Peter, with engaging frankness, announced loudly that they could each have TWO animals to take home, but not until they had eaten all the other things up. So they all set to with a will.

Then followed the ceremony of lighting the candles, and the children (including Peter himself) joined with enthusiasm in singing "Happy Birthday to You."

Tea was served promptly at four-fifteen. The menu consisted of :

Lettuce sandwiches

Buttered buns   *Biscuits*

Birthday cake

Ice cream and orange jelly

Milk

The party was a complete success. The children enjoyed it and their mothers did too. There were no temper tantrums, no upset stomachs, no nightmares to spoil the party, even in retrospect.

The party was brief, the group small. Games and decorations were not over-stimulating, and the food was simple. Mothers were present but unobtrusive.

These are the essentials of any happy party for such young children. Playing with the presents and toys, a game or two, a story or some music before the meal, are all that a three-year-old can manage emotionally in a comparatively new social situation.

If you do not want to follow Peter's party exactly, you will find some other games for children of this age in Chapter 14.

3

Rosemary's Fourth Birthday

ROSEMARY'S mother let her enthusiasm run away with her when the time came for her daughter's first party. Cousin Peggy had to be invited, and cousins Tom and Jimmy. And, of course, there were the ten children in Rosemary's group at nursery school. She loved every single one of them, and it would not be fair not to have all of them.

That made fourteen with Rosemary—a large group for a party of children from three to five years of age. Oh well, some might not be able to come; and if they all should happen to arrive, what did it matter? Birthdays come only once a year. After all, the children were not asked until three-thirty. Some would certainly be late, and the first to put in an appearance would probably amuse themselves for half an hour or so. Then at four o'clock the gifts would be opened, and the children would play with them for a while. At four-thirty there would be the peanut hunt. Tea would be served at five, and at five-thirty the mothers would be at the front door ready to collect the children.

It was all very simple.

Having considered and disposed of the possible complications, Rosemary's mother set off with a clear conscience to buy a Jack Horner Pie, gay little matching favours, colourful paper hats and amusing trinkets as prizes for the peanut hunt.

But you know what happens to the best-laid plans of mice and mothers. Every child accepted the invitation with great glee. At a quarter past three the doorbell began ringing. Ten minutes later the house was a bedlam. Excited children were running through the rooms. The wrappings had been torn from all the gifts. Puzzles and parts of playthings were scattered everywhere.

When the last guest arrived at three-thirty, Rosemary ran to the door before anyone else could get there, grabbed the neatly tied package from under her startled guest's arm, dashed into the room and shouted: "I've got another present!"

Long ago the peanuts had all been found, eaten, and the shells strewn all over the floor. It was the peanuts that started the trouble—they and the lack of something definite to do at the very beginning of the party.

For a moment Rosemary's mother was panic-stricken. Her daughter had never behaved so badly; neither had any of the other children when she had seen them individually. Fortunately, she did some quick thinking, and, with the help of some friends who had come to look on, rescued the party from complete chaos.

One of the adults unearthed a picture book, and soon had an entranced audience of three of the more shy children who had almost been overwhelmed by the excitement. A little boy who seemed to be confused by the crowd, and yet did not want to hear the story, was asked if he would like to listen to Rosemary's gramophone in the next room. He accepted the suggestion eagerly and spent half an hour having a lovely party by himself.

That left ten high-spirited boys and girls growing more wildly excited every minute while doing nothing. Rosemary's mother suggested *London Bridge*. In a few seconds the children were happily playing the game. *Did you ever see a Lassie?* and *Mulberry Bush* followed. After the circle games, the children sat on the floor and made up games from well-known nursery rhymes and children's songs. The entire group sang while several of the children took turns in acting the part of the Spider and Miss Muffet, the cat who went to London, Jack and Jill, and Bo-Peep.

Tea was served fifteen minutes earlier than originally planned. The children were completely relaxed now. The table looked so pretty in the softly lighted room. The meal of lettuce and tomato sandwiches, little cakes, jellies and ice cream, and, of course, the birthday cake, was so tasty that everyone was happy, and the children behaved like the charming little angels their mothers had hoped they would be.

After tea, Rosemary's mother gathered all the children round the fireplace in the living-room, and sang songs and read stories to them, Meanwhile, her adult friends took care of the amenities of greeting the parents as they came to take their children home.

As usual, there was a post-mortem after the party. You can probably guess the decision. Never Again! Not "never again" to parties, but to such a large group, to such a long party for children under five, to expecting fourteen children to amuse themselves in a city house arranged for adult living and not for child playing.

The party that finally evolved was very satisfactory, but it followed a hectic beginning and some anxious moments for Rosemary's mother. If you would benefit from her experience, limit the length of the party to an hour and a half at the longest. Have toys, puzzles, picture books, and, if possible, some music to entertain the first arrivals as well as the children who may not yet be ready for group play. Be prepared with games or pastimes for every unoccupied moment. (Many games for four-year-olds are given throughout this book.)

Precede the meal with a quiet activity, and plan something relaxing for the children to do while they are waiting for their parents to come for them.

4

An A·B·C Party

The 4–6 year-olds

A IS for *apple*; B is for *bunny*. If your little boy or girl is just becoming acquainted with the A B C—those funny signs that are strung together to spell people's names, or the words in the wonderful stories mother reads, why not give him an A B C party for his birthday?

Your invitation can be this Mother Goose rhyme, slightly altered for the occasion:

A B C
Tumble Down D
Come to my Party
And Play with Me.

Write the invitation on plain note-paper and paste cut-out alphabet letters round it in gay disarray. The letters can be purchased in most stationery stores. You will want several sizes, small ones for the invitations and larger ones for the games.

Some Games to Play

Pinning Letters

A new version of the old stand-by, *Pinning the Tail on the Donkey*, is a good game to play with the first arrivals.

With adhesive tape (which comes off without leaving a trace), attach a large piece of white cardboard to the wall at one end of the room. On the cardboard draw the outlines of an open book, and on the pages print in large letters the first initial of each child's name.

Cut matching letters from cardboard. Give one to each of the children and let them take turns at pinning letters in the book.

The one who, while he is blindfolded, pins his letter nearest the corresponding letter on the cardboard wins the game.

Instead of tying a handkerchief or a piece of cloth over the child's eyes, slip a paper bag over his head. It is easier to handle and makes a more effective blindfold.

A B C Hunt

Conceal a large assortment of alphabet letters round the room and let the children hunt for them. Provide each child with a paper bag in which to carry the letters he finds.

Play the game for ten or fifteen minutes. Then call the children together and let them sit on the floor or round the table to count their findings.

Alphabet Pictures

After going to the trouble of digging them out of all the nooks and crannies in the house, the children will want to keep the letters they find. What could be more fun than to let each child use his collection to make an alphabet picture to take home to his mother?

If the letters are gummed, the picture-making is very simple. The only equipment you will have to provide for each child is a piece of bright kindergarten paper about 5 or 6 in. in size, a saucer of water, and a small sponge or piece of cloth. With these accessories the little artists will soon be at work producing pictures of great skill and originality.

If paste must be applied to the letters, some precautions are necessary. The simplest way of handling this particular make-something game is to place in front of each child a folded newspaper on which he can spread his letters. Apply paste to the letters yourself, and let the children arrange them on the kindergarten paper in any way they like.

Give a prize for the best picture and one for the neatest.

Five Little Chickadees[1]

All A B C's and no numbers make Jack a one-sided boy. So follow the letter games with this 1-2-3-4-5 game which children have played for generations.

Five litt-le chick-a-dees, peep-ing at the door.

One flew a-way and then there were four.

Chorus:

Chick-a-dee, chick-a-dee, Happy and gay.

Chick-a-dee, chick-a-dee, Fly a way.

[1] The words for this game are taken from *The Song Play Book*, by Crampton and Wollaston, and are used with the permission of the publishers, A. S. Barnes & Co.

The players walk round the circle singing:

1. Five little chickadees,
   Peeping at the door;
   One flew away
   And then there were four.

   Chorus:
   Chickadee, chickadee,
   Happy and gay;
   Chickadee, chickadee,
   Fly away.

2. Four little chickadees,
   Sitting on a tree;
   One flew away
   And then there were three.

3. Three little chickadees
   Looking at you;
   One flew away
   And then there were two.

4. Two little chickadees,
   Sitting in the sun;
   One flew away
   And then there was one.

5. One little chickadee,
   Left all alone;
   It flew away
   And then there were none.

Choose five children to be the chickadees. The other children form a circle round the chickadees. If the group is small and there are not enough children left to form a circle, reduce the number in the centre to three, and start the game with the third verse.

Each chickadee in the centre has a number. When the time comes to "fly away," the one whose turn it is to leave the centre runs round the room. The others follow. They continue "flying" until the end of the chorus. Then they join hands with the runaway chickadees and re-form the circle for the next verse. After the last child in the centre has joined the outside circle, choose new chickadees and repeat the game from the beginning.

Honey-Pots

The children squat down and clasp their hands under their bended knees. You are the shop-keeper selling pots of honey. Another adult or an older child is the buyer. The buyer looks over the honey-pots and decides to buy the one that weighs the most. To decide the weight, you and the buyer take each of the children, one by one, lift them under the arms and swing them back and forth. Each pot weighs as many pounds as the number of times you can swing the child before he has to unclasp his hands.

Perhaps the game ought to be called *Giggling Honey-Pots*. It's an old, old favourite, but a very amusing one, and it entertains the children endlessly.

Signal Man

A variation of the always popular *Musical Chairs* is fun to play just before tea. You won't need a piano or gramophone for this version.

The children march round a line of chairs. There should be one chair less than the number of children playing, and they should be facing in alternate directions. An older child or an adult takes the part of the signal man, who stands in the centre holding a cane and chants:

Take your seats as soon as you can,
When you're called by the Signal Man!

When he taps three times the children scramble for seats. The one who does not get a chair is eliminated from the game. Remove a chair each time, and continue playing until there is only one chair left. The child who succeeds in getting that one wins the game.

The Party Table and Tea

A B C D E F G,
The birthday cake we're going to see.
H I J K L M N O P,
Come to the table now with me.

The birthday cake deserves this musical introduction. It is a very pretty pink cake with A B C biscuits pressed into the frosting all round the sides, and a row standing on end—outlining the edge of the top layer. The biscuits are covered with snowy-white icing, to match the candles in the centre.

At each child's place is a pink paper cup filled with white sweets. The place-cards attached to the handles read: "J is for John"; "L is for Leslie." Favours are sixpenny colouring books and a box of crayons for each child.

The tea menu consists of:

Sandwiches cut into A B C shapes
Small buns Biscuits
Birthday cake
Ice cream and fruit salad
Milk or lemonade

5
A MODEL RAILWAY PARTY

[For boys from six to ten years]

WHAT young Bill Jones ever had trains, rails, and points enough to satisfy his imagination? Even if the family budget could stand the strain of buying the entire L.M.S. system in miniature, the boys I know would still dream of wider horizons for their railways.

Every now and then two or three boys will pool their trains and build a railway that is almost as big as their dreams. For these boys there could be no more exciting party than one to which their friends were invited to bring their trains and set up a system that would rival Clapham Junction at holiday time.

An appropriate invitation for such a party could be made by the host himself, something on the following lines:

STOP !

A Railway Party's Coming !

I am inviting my friends to bring

their rails and trains to my house

next Saturday.

Don't fail to be there when the

whistle blows at four!

Every person will recognize his own engine and coaches even if there are a hundred more just like them. He would have to be a wizard, however, to sort a jumbled pile of rails and distribute the proper sections to ten or more owners. Before the boys add theirs to the general collection therefore, let them mark each section with some distinguishing identification. Pieces of different-coloured string will serve the purpose.

The young engineers will be perfectly happy playing with their trains for an hour or more. But, since this is a party as well as a gathering of railroad hobbyists, plan a few lively games to climax the afternoon's play with the right spirit of fun and fellowship.

Engine Toss

Fasten the picture of a train, mounted on cardboard, to some kind of stand. The picture can be taken from a magazine. A quart-size milk bottle makes a good support. You will also need eight quoits or rubber washers.

The game is played like this: Two players constitute a team. Each boy has four rings, and the competitors take turns in tossing them at the figure. There are no "ringers," but the "leaners" count three points. If none of the rings touch the figure, the nearest to it scores one point. Have a ruler handy to measure distances. Sometimes there are arguments about whose is closest. No point is scored in the case of a tie.

When there are more than three teams, provide additional equipment, so that the players do not have to wait too long between turns.

Broken-down Engine

An uproarious game follows. Form two teams of five or six players. If the group is smaller, eliminate one of the rôles to be performed. If it is larger, form additional teams. Players line up in single file behind a starting line. Teams are parallel. Number the players and assign to them the following rôles:

1. Cracked whistle—Imitate the sound of a locomotive whistle.

2. Broken wheel—Limp across the room.

3. Open switch—Jump across the room.

4. Shaky trestle—Since the engine has to proceed very slowly, the player crawls on all fours.

5 and 6. Double engine on a steep grade—The last player locks his arms round the fifth boy's waist, and the two walk together.

This is a walking race in which the teams compete against each other. Corresponding numbers on each side perform the same action. Blow a whistle to start. As soon as it sounds, all the Number One players walk as fast as they can across the room and back, while doing their best to imitate the shrill whistle of a locomotive approaching a busy crossing. When they return to the starting line, they touch the hand of the second player in their team. He starts limping immediately. The game ends when the last player in any group gets back to the starting line. His team is winner.

Engine Puzzles

After this uproarious interlude, a quieter game is in order. An engine picture puzzle fills the bill perfectly. Make the puzzles before the party by mounting pictures of engines on cardboard. Cut each one into small pieces of various shapes, and place in an envelope. When the time for the game arrives, distribute the envelopes to the boys. If they do not finish assembling the pictures before tea, they can continue putting them together while waiting to be called for, or can complete them at home.

THE TEA TABLE

A setting which is in keeping with the railway theme can be easily arranged by running a length of rail down the centre of the table, placing Tommy's engine (which you can retrieve at the last minute) in the middle, and standing signal posts at each end.

At each child's place have one of these engine-driver's caps which will make your young guests look as if they are ready to "mount into the cabin."

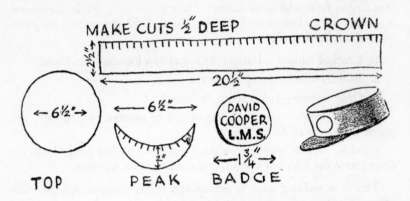

Crown.—Top: Cut a circle of blue kindergarten paper 6½ in. in diameter. Band: Cut a strip 20½ in. long and 2½ in. wide, making ½-in. notches all along one 20½ in. length. Paste band together, ends overlapping ½ in., then fold the cut notches in towards centre, and paste the crown on top.

Peak.—With same 6½ in. diameter cut a half-circle; then from points A and B cut a sector 2 in. at widest point C. Make ½-in. notches along inner edge. Bend notches and paste inside cap band.

Badge.—A circle 1¾ in. diameter. On it write the name of railway and boy's name. Paste to cap band.

The caps and signal posts are simple enough for the young host to make. If you want to indulge in a little extravagance, give each boy a toy signal lantern. It can either have a tiny electric bulb inside, or be filled with sweets.

Suggested Menu

Sausage rolls	*Tomato sandwiches*
Cream buns	*Biscuits*

Chocolate cake
Ice cream and jellies
Milk or lemonade

A Doll Party

6

[For girls from four to eight years]

"I WANT Annabelle. I must find her. I think she must be in your house."

Four-year-old Susan was at my door asking for her doll. A hurried search revealed the lost doll. Susan clutched it to her, stroked its hair, smoothed its dress, and deluged the doll with maternal questions. After a while she looked up and said,

"I'm glad to have Annabelle again. She said she likes being here."

It was a touching compliment. I had forgotten, as most grown-ups seem to, how very important their favourite dolls are to little girls of four, five or six years old. Then and there I decided that the next time I planned a party for children of this age, it was going to be a Doll Party.

The invitation is a very simple one in jingle style, which children love:

Dear Barbara,

    I'm going to have a party.
    My dolly's coming too.
    I hope you'll come and play with me,
    And bring your dolly too.

                  Susan Payne

25 Park Avenue   *September 12th, 4-5.30*

When the little guests arrive, remember that each one is bringing her very dearest friend. Greet both of them. Ask the doll's name. Comment on its hair, its clothes, its size, or any other attributes of which you think its owner might be especially proud. The little girls themselves will go on from where you leave off. And those first few minutes —which are so hard to plan—will be filled with the busy chatter of children showing off their dolls and making them perform in their best company manner.

If the party is to celebrate a birthday, take the gifts the children bring, and explain that Susan (or whichever little girl is having the party) is going to keep the packages together and open them later. Opening presents usually comes first, but children so young as this cannot admire presents and dolls at the same time. So keep one, preferably the presents, in reserve.

When the last guest has put in her appearance, you are ready for the treat that makes this quite the nicest party a little girl could imagine. Present each child with a gaily beribboned box containing some scraps of lace and long pieces of cloth; a bunch of artificial flowers; a paper of pins; a collection of large-holed beads for necklaces, with round shoe-laces for stringing; and several pieces of ribbon for sashes and hair-ribbons.

You probably won't need to explain that these are to be used to adorn the dolls and make them even prettier for the party. Also don't be surprised if the girls bedeck themselves as much as the dolls.

Prizes are not necessary, but if you decide to give them, arrange that each child receives one. You might stage a doll fashion-show, and give prizes for the largest doll, the smallest, the one with the longest curls, the most life-like doll, the one that sounds like a real baby when it cries, and the one wearing the prettiest outfit or necklace made at the party.

OPENING THE GIFTS

The children will want to see the gifts before tea. Their curiosity is sure to get the better of them after a little while. Besides, there is too little time following the meal to admire new toys and playthings properly.

Allow fifteen minutes for this part of the party. Follow it with games if tea is not yet ready.

To avoid confusion, ask the children to put their dolls on chairs pushed back against the wall; or better still, on a table from which the dolls can see the presents too. Unless you make this suggestion, you may find that some little miss will hold up the entire party by insisting that her doll have a turn in playing with the new toys or trying on the new hair-bows.

GAMES TO PLAY

The games start with the old favourite, *Here we go round the Mulberry Bush,* properly arrayed to do honour both to the dolls and to the little hostess.

You probably remember the game from your own childhood. The players walk round in a circle singing the chorus, which starts the game and repeats after each verse. During the verse the children stand still and go through the motions suggested by the words they are singing.

> *Chorus:* We've come to see Miss Susan Payne,
> Miss Susan Payne, Miss Susan Payne,
> We've come to see Miss Susan Payne,
> And how is she to-day?

> 1. Susan is washing her dolly's clothes,
> Her dolly's clothes, her dolly's clothes,
> Susan is washing her dolly's clothes,
> So early Monday morning.

> 2. Susan is ironing her dolly's clothes, etc.,
> So early Tuesday morning.

3. Susan is mending her dolly's clothes, etc.,
   So early Wednesday morning.

4. Susan is sweeping her dolly's floor, etc.,
   So early Thursday morning.

5. Susan is baking her dolly's bread, etc.,
   So early Friday morning.

6. Susan is scrubbing her dolly's floor, etc.,
   So early Saturday morning.

7. Susan is taking her dolly to church, etc.,
   So early Sunday morning.

If the children wish to play the game again, substitute their names for Susan's, using a different name in each verse. Slur the syllables in the names to make them fit, if they are longer than the song requires. Girls of this age are very fond of singing games, so they may want to try another. Try *Did you ever see a Lassie?* as described in the chapter on games. Substitute the word "dolly" for "lassie." Suggest that the children perform as their dollies might do—walk stiff-legged, bow, cry "Mama."

Of What am I Thinking?

After such an active game the children will be ready for this quieter one, described in Easter Party. One modification should be made when the children are under six or seven years of age. Instead of letting the children take turns in thinking out the questions, the adult should ask all of them. The first child to guess what you are thinking about scores one point.

To make the game more exciting, mark the score in large numerals on a blackboard or on a large sheet of paper.

Of Whom am I Talking?

A good game to play, either with the whole group before tea, or after the meal with any of the children whose parents may not be able to call for them promptly, is *Of Whom am I Talking?* You start it by saying:

> *Someone I know* has lost her sheep,
> And can't tell where to find them.
> Of whom am I talking?

By the time you get to the question the children will probably be shouting, "Bo-Peep! Bo-Peep!"

Go through their favourite nursery rhymes and poems, reciting part of each, and asking the question in the same way each time.

THE TEA TABLE

A delightful surprise awaits the little girls in the dining-room. In one corner is a special table, nursery-size, set just for their dolls. On it are tiny place cards and favours and a centrepiece exactly matching those on the bigger table round which the children are going to sit. This is sure to be a great and wonderful occasion, so allow the little girls plenty of time to seat their dolls, arrange their dresses, and to give them last-minute lectures on table manners. Four and five year olds take their maternal duties very seriously. Susan said to Annabelle: "Now you be good and eat your cake, and don't 'rupt other people when they're talking."

If you don't have enough chairs for the dolls, use toy bricks or boxes; or place an unopened card table on the floor and arrange cushions round it.

The centrepiece is a shimmering cellophane doll which reflects rainbow colours from the lights in the room. These attractive figures can be varied to fit many themes. The doll described here carries a handkerchief bouquet to match the favours, but you can make a bonnet and substitute a watering-can for the nosegay, and you have a charming Mistress Mary for the centrepiece. The figures for both the children's and the dolls' tables are constructed in exactly the same way. The measurements for each are as follows:

	LARGE DOLL	SMALLER DOLL
Inside cellophane fold	9 ft. by 17 in.	4 ft. by 9 in.
Cellophane square for head	10 in.	6 in.
Peach crêpe square for head	10 in.	6 in.
Cellophane straws	$1\frac{1}{2}$ boxes 18 in. long	1 box 10 in. long
Size of head	$2\frac{1}{2}$ in. by 2 in.	$1\frac{1}{2}$ in. by 1 in.
Lace doily for bouquet	4 in.	4 in.
Blue crêpe paper for handkerchief	7 in. by 7 in.	5 in. by 5 in.

Make the head first by pressing a roll of cotton-wool into the required shape. Stretch the square of peach crêpe paper tautly over the cotton-wool. Be sure there are no folds in the paper, and that the face is smooth.

Now pull the square of cellophane over the head, smooth it carefully over the face, and tie the folds together at the neck. Loosely fold the large piece of cellophane, and pink one edge to eliminate any possible bulkiness.

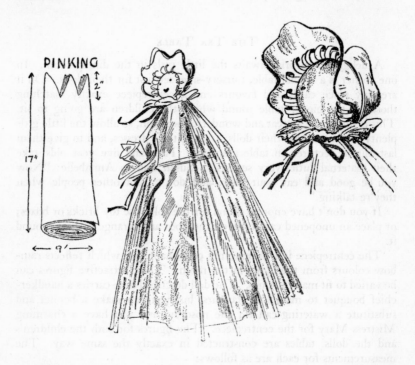

Gather the pinked edge and tie it round the neck with hat wire. The inside fold should be full and unwrinkled, so that the figure will stand firmly.

Now separate the straws into four piles. With one hand clasp the doll round the neck. With the other, pick up one pile of straws at a time, transfer them to the hand holding the doll, and distribute them evenly round the body. The straws should be grasped about an inch from the end. Tie tightly with wire, and the shorter ends will spread out to form a graceful frill round the neck.

Cut a strip of crêpe paper for the hair. Fringe one side, and roll the whole strip over a small knitting needle. The fringe will curl and the strip can then be shaped over the head. The doll in the illustration has bangs as well as yellow neck curls.

The hat is made from a semicircular piece of blue crêpe paper (8 in. in diameter for the larger, 5 in. for the smaller doll), pleated at the back. The mouth is a tiny gummed heart, and the eyes are blue half-circles.

To make the bouquet favours, cut a cross in the centre of the lace-paper doily. Insert cotton handkerchiefs in the children's nosegays, and crêpe paper squares in the dolls' bouquets. The diagram shows how to fold the squares.

FOLD   FOLD   ROLL

After the handkerchief has been inserted into the doily, wrap the stem portion with tinfoil, tie a narrow ribbon bow under the frill, and your nosegay will look like this:

7 *For the 4-5 & 6 year olds*
A HALLOWE'EN PARTY

IF it is Hallowe'en, and you are planning a party, darken the room, festoon the lights with orange streamers, and dangle black cats from the ceiling. Fill your flower vases with autumn leaves, and place jack-o'-lanterns on the mantel and the window-sills.

You may be bored with these traditional trappings, but to a very little boy or girl a Hallowe'en party without them would be as disappointing as a Christmas morning without a Christmas tree.

Let the little host help you cut out the turnip or pumpkin faces. That's half the fun of a Hallowe'en party. Give the jack-o'-lanterns silly grins or clownish looks rather than fierce expressions. Whatever you do, save the ghosts and toothless witches for later years. The spooky doings in which adults revel will terrify most small children. Games or decorations which are in any way startling or macabre should be excluded from all parties for boys and girls under twelve. Even after that they should be introduced only in small doses.

INVITATION

In keeping with the spirit of the occasion, choose invitations which are excitingly mystifying to the little guests. This one has no name. The child who receives it must figure out—with the aid of his mother, of course—who has sent it. The map gives the only clue. But since the address is under the house, mother will usually know at a glance who the host is to be. In the larger cities, where mothers do not always know the house numbers of their children's friends, it might be well to write the sender's name in small letters in one corner of the invitation.

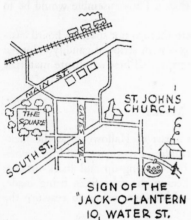

SIGN OF THE "JACK-O-LANTERN 10, WATER ST.

The invitations can be written on correspondence cards on which ready-made cut-outs are pasted; or you can make your own from orange kindergarten paper cut in the shape of a pumpkin lantern. (Here is another way in which the little host can help you in the party preparations.)

Fold the kindergarten paper so that you have a double sheet the size you need for each lantern. Leave the left side uncut, so that the lantern will open like a book. Cut out the first one, and let the child take care of the rest. If the shapes are not perfect, so much the better. That's the charm of home-made things.

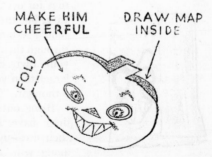

MAKE HIM CHEERFUL   DRAW MAP INSIDE

FOLD

With black ink, draw the features of a grinning jack-o'-lantern on the outside. Trace the map inside. If you use carbon paper you can do three or four at a time.

DRESSING-UP

In the party room, have a trunk or several large boxes brimming over with dress-up treasures with which the children can make themselves into kings and fairies, cowboys or pirates, or any other wonderful people of story-book land. Cast-off curtains, brightly coloured shoes and hats, beach wraps, gaudy sashes, ribbons, out-moded evening dresses, discarded bracelets and necklaces, feather and flower hat trimmings—these are the accessories from which children assemble fashion creations which are more wonderful to them than a Paris ensemble would be to their mothers.

If you happen to live in a flat where there is not space to hoard cast-offs for such an occasion, fill your boxes with strips of gaudily coloured cottons and muslins, or rolls of crêpe paper. These substitute materials can be bought at small cost.

MAKING MASKS

Costumes and masks are as much a part of Hallowe'en as the jack-o'-lanterns. But because some small children experience real fright when they first see others in false-faces, the dressing-up and mask-making should be part of the party itself. Seeing the false-faces being made, and having a share in creating one of his own, seems to reassure the timid child.

The masks are made of large white paper bags. Those with flat bottoms are best. There should be one for each child, plus a few extras to replace any that might be torn. Before the party starts, cut the open-

ings for eyes, nose, and mouth. Shapes may vary, but the eye openings in all the false-faces should be large enough for the children to see through them without difficulty. Try one on your own child first. Children's heads are larger than you think—or, at least, larger than I thought.

Bring out the paper bags when the children have finished arraying themselves in their dress-up finery. Give one to each child along with a box of crayons, and let them decorate the masks. The children should be seated round a low table to do this. If you have not one large enough, let them do their crayoning on the floor. Help the spirit of fun by making a mask for yourself.

GAMES TO PLAY

Now that the children are masked and costumed, there must be a parade—a follow-the-leader one, with all kinds of twists and turns. Lead it yourself to piano or gramophone music.

Hallowe'en Blind Man's Buff

Following the exciting parade, the children sit in a circle for a quieter game. One child is chosen "It." He stands in the centre with his mask turned backwards so that he cannot see.

Ask the other children to be very quiet until you point to one of them. The child you have singled out says, "Hello, Mr. Mask-Man." "It" tries to guess by the voice who asked the question. If he is not successful, he is allowed two more guesses. If any of them are correct, the child who spoke takes "It's" place in the centre; otherwise "It" chooses someone to replace him.

Giant in the Ring

Before playing this game, ask the children to remove their masks. Write on each one the name of the child who made it, so that you can return the mask to its owner before he goes home.

One of the players is chosen to be the "giant" who is locked in a castle and is trying to escape. The castle is a ring which children form by clasping hands firmly. The "giant" may scamper from one side of the circle to the other. He may crawl under the children's joined hands, or try to break them apart by pushing against them. But he may not hang on to the children's arms or push into their bodies.

Anyone who lets the giant out of the castle must take his place. Should there be a question as to which child was responsible, choose the one to the right of the space through which the giant made his escape.

Apples on a String

At least one traditional game must be included in the programme if the Hallowe'en party is to be a complete success. This one is an excellent choice for small children.

Tie a stout cord across the room and attach to it four vertical strings. These should be 2 ft. or more apart, and should hang just to the tops of the children's heads. Loop the free ends and slip each one over the stem of an apple.

Four children, with their hands behind their backs, line up in front of the apples and try to bite into them. The first to succeed wins, but each competitor receives his own apple. It's the first course of the party meal.

Suspend four more apples on the strings and let other children compete.

THE TEA TABLE

Centrepiece

Since this is a Hallowe'en party, you will certainly want a lantern centrepiece made from a pumpkin or large swede. Make him a roguish fellow, with slices of cucumber for ears, a red beet for his nose, small white sweets for teeth, and celery or carrot-top hair.

Favours

A pumpkin-faced scarecrow, with a name card in one hand and his other dipped into a paper cup filled with sweets, makes an amusing place-card favour. These entertaining favours are so easy to make that the little host can do most of the work himself.

First paste a strip of black crêpe paper, $1\frac{1}{2}$ in. wide and 7 in. long, round a paper cup, 2 in. in diameter across the top. Flute the edge of the paper. Then paste the cup in the centre of a piece of orange kindergarten paper, 3 in. by 4 in. in size. If you want a firmer base, back the kindergarten paper with cardboard. Fill the cup with sweets.

You will need two 6-in. and one $5\frac{1}{2}$-in. pipe cleaners for the body of the scarecrow. Hold them together, and force the three through a green cellophane straw, 2 in. in length. Centre the straw to form the body of the figure. Pull up the shorter pipe cleaner until only half an inch extends from the bottom of the straw. Bend this back to make the tail. Bend the other end of the same cleaner at right angles to the top of the straw. This forms the arm which holds the place card. Bend the third straw in the opposite direction to make the longer arm which dips into the sweets.

Cover arms and legs with green cellophane straws cut into the required length. Leave a short section of the legs free to form feet. Paste these to the orange paper just behind the paper cup. Shape the legs and bend the body into position.

Now paste a pumpkin-face cut-out on the section of pipe cleaner which protrudes above the body, and your grinning scarecrow will be impatient for the party to begin.

MENU

Small meat pâtés   Lettuce and tomato salad

Orange layer cake   Funny-face biscuits

Milk or orangeade

Apples   Crackers

8
RAINY DAY DRESS-UP

LIKE Topsy, some of the best parties "just grow." Don't you remember the rainy days when you and your friends raided the trunk in the attic for mother's first party dress, a piece of lace from grandmother's shawl, and an old 1890 leghorn hat with red cabbage roses? Sometimes when we were left alone we ventured farther and borrowed the bedspreads and table-covers for the sweeping capes we needed. Once or twice, too, mother's best felt hat mysteriously found its way to the attic, to be used on such occasions.

Most of us were girls, so we were usually queens and princesses. When the boys of the neighbourhood came to play, we had to be Cowboys and Indians or Knights of the Round Table. Our younger sisters went modern when their turn came, and held fashion shows or pretended that they were glamorous film stars.

46

To-day's children, in their just-pretend play, are Snow White, Lone Rangers, aviators, or war lords. Rôles vary as the years pass. Yet no matter how much they change externally, the inherent joy of make-believe remains the same for the children of each generation.

Modern living has squeezed the rambling attic from most homes. But somewhere in every house there is a corner big enough for a dress-up treasure-chest. Keep it filled. From time to time replace over-used accessories with tempting new ones. Bring out the chest on rainy days or during the hot summer, then leave the children to themselves.

In their just-pretend world, children stretch their imaginations, throw off adult restrictions, and like François Villon become kings for a day. Yours must be the rôle of the silent partner. No matter how hard you try, you cannot enter this part of the children's world. They may assign to you some particular part to play when they need an extra character, but it is strictly on their own terms. If you insist on intruding farther, you dispel the magic and the game breaks up.

So retire to the kitchen, and have the fun of playing your own game of fairy princess by concocting some toothsome surprise for the children. One of the greatest delights of our dress-up games was to have mother suddenly appear with a pitcher of ice-cold lemonade and a plate of ginger-snaps. We were queens and this was a royal feast.

Some rainy day, when you wish to give the children a very special treat, surprise them with a real party meal served at the table. Place a crêpe-paper-covered watering-can in the centre. Flute the edges of the paper, and fill the can with flowers from your garden. On each child's plate lay a colourful handkerchief umbrella (which you have made previously and stored away for just such a rainy day). Serve simple tea sandwiches or biscuits and a fruit drink.

To make the umbrella, wrap a narrow strip of bias-cut crêpe paper round a 12-in. piece of wire. Bend into shape, gather the handkerchief round the wire, and tie with a ribbon bow.

9

FOR CHILDREN OF 4-10

A CHRISTMAS PARTY

CHRISTMAS is a happy season for all the world. For children it is the most thrilling time of the whole year. The joy of Christmas will remain as the years pass and the child grows up. But never again will he be quite so eager, so filled with wonder as in the days when Santa Claus is real, and the reindeer dash down from the skies with their gift-laden sleigh.

Let's make the little children's Christmas, then, a sparkle of fun and laughter. Christmas Day belongs to the family. It is one of its most intimate and lasting joys. But sometime during the week following, or early in January, let the child share his happiness with his contemporaries —the little people who speak his language.

Write the invitation in white ink on a letter-size piece of red kinder-garten paper, and let the child who is having the party paste round it green cut-outs of stars and Christmas trees.

CHRISTMAS FUN

A guessing game opens the party and entertains the first arrivals. All the games are suitable for children of six years and over. Younger children will enjoy the simpler ones.

Santa went to the Grocer's

Start the game by saying, "Santa went to the grocer's and he bought some ———." The children try to guess what the purchase was. They may ask questions which can be answered by "Yes" or "No." "Was it something to drink?" "To wear?" The first child to guess correctly chooses the next object. If all the players are six years or older, give the initials of the object. "Santa went to the grocer's and he bought some c—— c——." The answer might be cherry cake, cream cheese, chopped celery.

Little Toy, What are You?

A blindfolded child walks round the room trying to touch one of the players. They taunt him by calling to him, but duck out of the way when he comes near. If he succeeds in getting close enough to touch one of the players, he says, "Little Toy, what are you?" The child whom he addresses may either make the sound of a toy, or tell Santa what it is. He may answer, "Toot, toot," or say, "I'm an engine." Santa tries to guess by the voice whom he has caught. If he is correct, the other child takes Santa's place. If his guess is wrong, he must be "It" again.

When the children do not know each other well enough to identify each other's voices, let them imitate the sounds of boats, trains, and other mechanical objects, and let Santa guess what they represent.

Drop the Bell

Form a single circle. Appoint one of the children to be "It" and give him a set of tinkling Christmas bells tied with a red ribbon. "It" walks round the circle, drops the bells on the floor behind one of the players, and runs back to his place in the circle. The child behind whom he drops the bells must pick them up quickly and try to tag "It" before he can get home. If he succeeds, "It" must take the bells again and go round the circle once more. If "It" gets back safely, the other child becomes "It."

Straddle Ball

Still in circle formation, the players stand with their feet touching. The player who had the bells at the end of the last game is "It" for this one. He stands in the centre and tries to roll a large, red rubber ball between the other players' legs. They try to prevent him from doing so by rolling it back toward him with their hands. If a player misses the ball and allows it to leave the circle, he takes "It's" place.

Treasure Trove

Wrap up a small prize with paper and string, making the knot easy to untie. Repeat this wrapping about half-a-dozen times.

The children sit round in a circle, facing inwards. Pass the wrapped parcel round the circle to music. The child who holds the parcel when the music stops undoes the outer wrapping. Allow only a very short interval, then start the music and pass the parcel again. At the second stop, the child holding the parcel undoes the next wrapping, and so on, until the last covering is undone. The child who uncovers the treasure keeps it as a prize.

Gift Maze

Because it is Christmas, and a party too, you will certainly want to give the children some inexpensive gifts. Hide them in corners and under the furniture in an adjoining room. Tie long strings to each one and twine the strings round table and chair legs. Lead them back and forth across the room. To the free ends attach tags on which the children's names are written. Explain that careful unravelling, not speed, will bring the quickest results. Avoid a complicated maze if the children are under seven.

THE PARTY TABLE

A small Christmas tree decorated with berries makes a perfect background for these jolly Christmas apples which beam at young guests. They are so simple to make that you can put them together in just a few minutes.

With cocktail sticks fasten marshmallow heads to shiny red apples. Insert two cloves in the face to represent eyes, and one for a mouth. Brush the cheeks with red vegetable colouring. Fasten cotton-wool hair and whiskers in place with egg-white.

The cocked red hat is a cone of red kindergarten paper. To make it, cut a 2¾-in. semicircle. Fold it so that the two halves of the diameter overlap. Paste these edges together.

MENU

Assorted sandwiches   *Small buttered pancakes*

Iced layer cake with Christmas decorations

Small cakes   *Chocolate biscuits*

Jellies   *Trifle*

Milk   Lemonade   Orangeade

Christmas Crackers

AFTER THE MEAL

Sing carols after supper. Even young children will enjoy favourites such as: *Hark! the Herald Angels Sing; O, Little Town of Bethlehem; Silent Night; The First Nowell; It Came Upon the Midnight Clear; Good King Wenceslas; Away in a Manger.*

An Easter Birthday Party

10

Come to my house next Tuesday,
And we'll have a hunting race
To find the eggs the bunny leaves
In his secret hiding-place.

Sheila Robinson

25 Avenue
Linden   *April 5, at 4 o'clock*

When you are not yet ten, Easter means wonderful chocolate confections, cuddly bunnies, and downy yellow chicks. It means eggs, too, lots of them. Eggs in all colours of the rainbow, some to eat, some to decorate; and, best of all, some to hunt and to find in the exciting old-fashioned make-believe game.

For this Easter birthday, pink or blue stationery, with a bunny cut-out in one corner, makes a very pretty come-to-my-party note. Some children will want to draw the bunnies all by themselves. Even those who have not yet learned to make their crayons and pencils behave will want some share in getting the invitations ready, and will have a wonderful time pasting ready-made cut-outs on the note-paper.

FOR AN INDOOR PARTY

The eggs must be hidden before the party starts—even from the young host, if that is possible. Chocolate eggs or jelly beans in tiny muslin or cellophane bags, or in nests of shredded paper, are best indoors. The lucky egg can be a larger chocolate one, or a hard-boiled egg painted gold. Before the hunt begins, be sure to explain that all the eggs are in plain sight. Nothing need be moved. This word of caution will save your house from being turned into a shambles. Children respect rules if they are made clear.

Hide enough eggs to make the hunt a real game. Have some in fairly obvious places and some in more obscure corners, so that the timid child and the go-getter will both have a fair chance. Provide each child with a small basket or a paper bag in which to place his treasures. (Mashed chocolate eggs are sticky decorations on rugs and furniture!)

The players hunt for ten minutes, or as long as they seem to be enjoying the search. When the time has come to end the search, call all the children together and let them sit in a circle, either on chairs or on the floor. Award prizes to the children who find the "lucky" chocolate or golden egg, the most eggs, and the greatest number of red, yellow, or blue eggs. Also have one or two prizes for the less lucky children.

Inexpensive toys, wrapped in crackling, glistening cellophane, make attractive gifts. Skipping-ropes, sets of bats and balls, kites, tops, and bags of marbles are prized acquisitions now that spring is in the air.

GAMES FOR INDOORS

Of What am I Thinking?

This is one of the most popular of guessing games. One child is chosen to be "It." He says, "I am thinking of something *pink*. What is it?" The others try to guess. The object chosen must be in the room. It may be Mary's hair-bow, or Lucy's sash, or a flower in a vase, or the window curtains. Whoever guesses correctly has the next turn to choose an object.

The Minister's Bunny

This word game—an Easter variation of *The Minister's Cat*—is a delight to boys and girls from six to ten who learned to manage their A B C's not so very long ago. Chairs are numbered and arranged in a line or a circle. The object of the game is to get into the first chair and to stay there as long as possible.

Starting with the letter "A," the children take turns in mentioning nouns or adjectives which describe the minister's bunny. The first one might say, "The minister's bunny is an *awful* bunny." The second might describe the minister's bunny as an *angry* bunny. The third child hesitates a moment, but then gets an inspiration and shouts, "The minister's bunny is an *artful* bunny." So far the minister's bunny is not a very high-class rabbit! But no matter how hard the fourth child tries, he cannot think of a single word starting with "A." If he does not succeed by the time you have counted "ten," he moves to the last seat, and the children below him move up one seat.

The child who was sitting next to the unlucky one, and is now in the seat he vacated, has the next turn. He mentions a word, but this time it must start with "B." Every time a child fails to think of a word and has to move, the letter changes. Older children like to continue until they have used every letter in the alphabet. Two or three times round the circle are generally enough for the younger ones.

Who has the Ring?

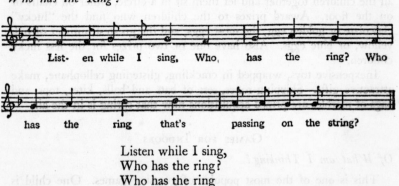

Listen while I sing,
Who has the ring?
Who has the ring
That's passing on the string?

A new tune brightens this old party favourite. A ring is placed on a string which is tied together at the ends. The string is just long enough so that all the players can place both hands on it while they are sitting close together in a circle. The child who is chosen to be "It" does not have a chair. He stands in the circle, while the other children sing the song to him and quickly pass the ring from one to the other. On the last word of the song the passing stops. "It" then tries to guess in whose hand the ring is hidden. If his guess is correct, the child holding the ring takes "It's" place. If the guess is incorrect, the song and passing are resumed and "It" tries again.

Outdoor Hunt

Dyed eggs are usually hidden outdoors, some singly, some in nests of two or three. If there are very young children in the group, pair them with older ones, and have a partner-hunt. Provide each child with a basket or paper bag in which to carry the eggs he finds. Define the limits in which the search is to be carried on, if the outdoor area is very large. To add zest to the game, announce before it starts that there are special prizes for the children who find the most eggs of one colour, and one for the child who finds the golden egg.

Let the game continue for fifteen minutes, or longer if the children are having fun. At the first sign of waning interest, however, blow a whistle or ring a bell as a signal that the hunt is over.

If the day is mild, let the children gather outdoors to count their eggs. Award prizes as suggested for the Indoor Hunt. After the children have admired each other's gaily coloured eggs and prizes, there will still be time for several outdoor games before tea is served. Ask them to place their bags or baskets on a table and play *Red Rover, Nose and Toe Tag, Find your Partner and Stoop*, all of which can be found in the List of Games.

Table Decorations

The party table is a special surprise. No fuzzy bunnies sit proudly in the centre, as they usually do at Easter parties. This is a very different kind of centrepiece, inexpensive, easy to assemble, yet so different that you are sure to hear a chorus of voices saying, "Oh, isn't that pretty!" while you lead your young guests into the dining-room.

The striking effect is achieved by two tiny angel figures which top the party cake, and by the unusual arrangement of glimmering yellow candles.

The cake, thickly covered with white icing, stands on a large cake plate, or on a circular board painted white or covered with white crêpe

paper. The candles, in flat white holders, are placed, not on the cake itself, but at 2-in. intervals round the edge of the plate or board. The candles are the 4-in. kind used on Christmas trees.

The angels are enchanting little figures, not at all home-made-looking. They can be made days ahead of the party, so that there is no last-minute flurry to worry you. After the party is over, you will find them graceful decorations for many other occasions, especially for Christmas and Easter holiday tables. Directions always sound complicated, but the illustrations will show you how easily the figures are put together.

To make the Angel Figures

Assemble your materials before you start to work. You will need eight 1-in. pastilles, two 1½-in. flat pastilles, two 1¾-in. circles of cardboard, two lollipop sticks, two pipe cleaners, two 8-in. squares of white glazed paper and about the same amount of gold kindergarten paper, a 10-in. square of clear cellophane, a narrow strip of yellow and a tiny piece of red and black crêpe paper.

The body consists of three 1-in. pastilles which stand one on top of the other on a larger pastille base. They are held together with a lollipop stick which extends about an inch above the top pastille.

Place a cardboard circle on one of the squares of glazed white paper, and stand the body on this cardboard base. Now gather the paper in folds round the body, and tie it together at the neck. Do not cut off the ends, but push them back so that they do not hide the face.

To make the head, place a fifth pastille on its side on the protruding lollipop stick. Wrap this pastille in cellophane and twist the ends together into a tight little spiral at the back of the head. The eyes are tiny dots of black crêpe paper; the mouth, a little curved piece of red paper. The curls are yellow crêpe paper. So is the little bonnet which frames the face. This is nothing more than a strip of crêpe paper the exact width of the pastille with the edges rolled under as shown in the diagram.

The arms are made from a single pipe cleaner. Twist the centre of it round the lollipop stick at the neck of the figure. The hymnal is a piece of gold cardboard or kindergarten paper 2¼ in. long and 2 in. wide. Crease it down the centre to make it look like a book, and paste the ends of the pipe cleaner to the outside edges.

Wings and halo are made of the same material as the hymnal. The halo is 1¼ in. in diameter, the wings 2¾ in. in width and 3¼ in. in length. The halo should be placed so that it will frame the angel's face. To achieve the proper angle, bend the part which is lettered "A" away from the halo, and paste this piece to the back of the head near the top. Insert the wings at the back of the neck underneath the spiral of cellophane which covers the face. Now your angels are ready to sing the joys of Eastertide!

Favours

At each child's place are little nests from which peep heads of bunnies and of saucy little maids in frilled yellow bonnets. These are combination favours and place cards. The nest itself is a white paper cup with

a yellow handle on which the child's name is written. Concealed inside are gold- and silver-wrapped sweets. Shredded green paper covers the sweets and provides the base from which the little heads peer over the top of the cup.

The heads are hard-boiled eggs. Those of the bunnies are white. The maids' heads are dyed pink. The features may be inked or painted. Tint the eyes of the bunnies pink, and the girls' eyes blue. Stiffen thin pieces of string in sugar water to make the bunnies' whiskers. A bit of cotton dipped in egg-white will hold them in place.

The maids' bonnets are made by pasting a strip of yellow crêpe paper round the egg. Flute the free edge of the paper and paste a bow at the chin.

MENU

Grated cheese and apple sandwiches
Assorted small cakes   *Chocolate biscuits*
Easter or Simnel cake
Fruit jellies   *Milk*   *Lemonade*
and Ice-cream Bunnies as a special treat

The ice cream should be frozen stiff, so that it will not melt while you are decorating the bunnies. Place a pink iced biscuit on each plate, and on the biscuit two spoonfuls of ice cream, one on top of the other. The top spoonful is the head of the bunny. Insert two long pink pastilles for ears, two small round ones for eyes, and long white pastilles cut into strips for whiskers. Cut the pastilles into the desired shapes before the time for serving. Then you can put the bunnies together in a few seconds.

11 SOAP BUBBLE PARTY

[For boys and girls from four to ten.]

THE July or August child is very lucky. His is a summer birthday which can be celebrated in enchanting ways which are not possible during the uncertain winter months.

Among the alluring choices are: picnics, beach parties, excursions, and, most exciting of all, a garden soap bubble party. It is such a perfect way in which to observe a birthday, that even the threat of a sudden shower cannot damp the festive spirit. At the first rumble of thunder, the party moves into the kitchen and continues as smoothly as if it had been planned that way.

Pink, blue, and yellow bubbles dance over the invitation. They are made by pasting circles of kindergarten paper on the note-paper or correspondence card on which the following verse is written:

Come to my house, my little friend,
The bubbles here will tell you when.
We'll blow some others into the air,
We know they'll float, but don't
* know where.*
But we can have a game to see
If yours or mine will bigger be.

When he arrives, each guest receives a package, as brightly done-up as any birthday gift. Inside is a clay pipe and a gaily-coloured rubber apron. Older children like the new bubble-blowers, but the younger set have more success with the old-fashioned pipes.

Once the children have donned their aprons, they can blow and spill without worrying for a moment about rumpling their best party clothes. The children's aprons, which are on sale at most of the stores for a few pence, will not completely cover the frocks or suits of older children, but they will provide all the protection that is needed. If aprons are unobtainable, suggest that mothers send their children in sun suits, which will dry quickly in the warm air. Neither host nor guests will have much fun if they have to fret over upsetting the bowls of soapy water, or dripping it from their pipes.

Each child should have his own bowl of water. Use metal bowls or clean tins instead of crockery dishes. The soapy water can be prepared beforehand and kept in quart jars or bottles. To get the best results, pour hot water over rich-lather soap flakes, and add a teaspoonful of glycerine to each quart of water. The glycerine makes the bubbles firmer.

Blowing bubbles is a magic feat. There's an endless fascination in making them, in watching the bubbles toss lightly in the breeze, in trying to understand what makes the colours as the sun shines on them. Most children will find enough pleasure in just doing this; but if you think that your guests would also like to play games, here are a number which fit very neatly into the bubble party theme:

Bubbles so High!

Stretch the string between two trees or posts, and let the children try to toss their bubbles over it. Older children like to blow bubbles across the string, but tiny tots cannot resist touching them with their hands once the bubbles start floating in the air. The game is better for them if they jerk the bubbles from their pipes over a string which is only slightly higher than their heads.

Whose is Biggest ?

Give each child a balloon—a rubber bubble which he can touch and play with. Award a prize to the child who blows up the biggest one. After this game you may want to blow the balloons a little higher and tie them with a string so that they can be played with more easily. Have a game to see which child can bat his balloon farthest without letting it touch the ground.

Magic Circles

Cut eight or ten large circles, and the same number of smaller ones, from cardboard or kindergarten paper. The circles should each be of a different colour. Place the smaller ones in a box, and scatter the large circles over the ground or floor. Tell the players that you are going to turn your back to them while they choose a circle on which to stand. Any number of players may stand on or round a circle. Also explain that before you turn round you are going to draw a smaller circle from the box you are holding. That is the magic circle, and the children who are standing on the larger one of corresponding colour will receive a prize. Penny lollipops are good awards for this game.

Replace the magic circle in the box. Allow the children to change places, and draw again.

Traffic Lights

Arrange the children along one side of a straight line, with a leader at one end. The leader directs the traffic. If he calls "red," the players run five paces behind the line; "green," five paces beyond the line. If he calls "amber," they must not move. By repeating the same order twice, the leader may trap the unwary. Players who do not obey directions must fall out of the game, and a small prize is awarded to the winner.

The Party Table

An outdoor picnic tea would be most appropriate for this type of party, but an indoor table can be set up beforehand without fear that a sudden gust of wind will blow away the decorations. And decorations are very important. It is the candles on the cake and the colours of the favours that make the meal a party in itself.

If you want your table to bubble with all the colours of the rainbow, cover it with crêpe paper, and paste multi-coloured paper circles all over the cover. Arrange a cluster of balloons in the centre of the table. Weight them with some heavy object. Tie the balloons separately, so that they can be detached after tea is over, and given to the children to take home.

For individual place-card holders, use these gay bubble stands. The base is a button mould, about an inch and a half in diameter, or a pastille.

The bubbles are marshmallows. Press them into bubble shape and cover with red and green cellophane. The strings are pieces of hat wire wrapped round the cellophane where it is gathered together. One is $5\frac{1}{2}$ in. in length, the other $4\frac{1}{2}$ in. Place the free ends inside a small cone of green cellophane, and force this into the opening in the base.

Menu

Sandwiches cut into circles
Birthday cake
Strawberries or raspberries and cream
Jellies   Ice cream

12

PETER PAN PICNIC

"*AND the still air is filled with the singing of birds and the ringing of hundreds of little fairy bells.*

"*But the sweetest sound of all is the fluting of Peter Pan's pipe, as he sits outside the little house and calls to the spring to make haste, because with the spring comes Wendy.*"

And so, when spring or summer brings a party to your little Wendy or Peter, make it an imaginary trip to the magic Neverland, to share with the Lost Boys those thrilling adventures which grown-ups "*can never, never have.*"

Run into your Cave

The Boys, you will remember, lived in a cosy cave, but whenever they ventured forth, they were in constant terror of the pirates who were skulking in the woods, ready to pounce on them and carry them off.

In this game, one of the Lost Boys is in the woods and is being chased by Captain Hook. Choose two players for their rôles, and then divide the others into groups of three. Two players in each set face each other and join hands to form the caves. The third stands between them.

Unfortunately, each cave is large enough for only one person. If the Lost Boy who is trying to escape Hook runs into a cave to seek refuge, the player who occupied it must vacate it immediately. Hook then pursues this Boy, and the only way he can escape is to dash into a different cave and expose one of the others to the terror of being chased by the malevolent Captain.

If Captain Hook catches any of the Lost Boys, he and the boy exchange places. Occasionally Hook may shout, "Cave's Afire." Then all the Lost Boys must run for different caves. Hook and the Boy without a home join the general scramble. If they succeed in getting into any of the vacated caves, the two players left without homes become the runner and pursuer.

Let the children take turns in representing the caves and the Lost Boys, so that everyone will have an opportunity to play tag with Hook.

Walking the Plank

"Yo ho! Yo ho! the frisky plank,
You walks along it so—
Till it goes down and you goes down
To Davy Jones below!"

Place a narrow plank on blocks, so that the plank is raised several inches from the ground. Have a game to see which children can walk its length, then turn round and walk back without falling off.

If you can't get a plank, let the children walk along a white string stretched taut on the ground. Players must place one foot in front of the other and not step off the string to regain their balance. Older children who can do the stunt easily will find walking the plank quite a trick if they have to do it while looking through the wrong end of a pair of field or opera glasses.

Peter and Hook (*Cat and Mouse*)

The villainous Hook was ever-present until his fateful duel on the pirate ship. Even though the Boys escaped him in the first game, he is again chasing Peter in this one.

The players join hands in a circle. One is chosen to be Peter; another, Hook. Peter stands inside the circle to start. Hook stands outside. The children in the circle try to prevent Hook from catching Peter. They may not drop hands, but they may lower them if Hook tries to crawl under, or raise them if he attempts to jump over the fence they are forming round Peter.

If by chance Hook should get inside the circle, they quickly let Peter out and try to keep Hook in. When Hook catches Peter, he takes Peter's place. Peter joins the children in the circle and chooses one of them to play the part of Hook.

Clock Hunt

"Tick tick! terrick, tick, tick!" When Hook heard that sound he fled in mortal fear of the crocodile that had swallowed the alarm clock.

The crocodile would not be a pleasant guest to have at a picnic, but the clock can be used in a merry hunting game. Choose a loud-ticking one with an alarm. While the children cover their eyes, hide it in some obscure spot. Set the alarm so that the clock will ring ten minutes later. Then let the children search for it. The Boy who finds the clock before the alarm rings wins an inexpensive prize.

After it has been found, call the children together and start once more from the beginning. Explain carefully the limits within which you will hide the clock, so that the children will not wander too far away.

Shadow Tag

All the Darlings' trouble started when Peter lost his shadow. What could be more appropriate, therefore, than a game of shadow tag for the children of Neverland?

One child is chosen to be "It." He tries to tag the others. They tempt him by running close, but when he gets near a player, the boy can save himself by casting his shadow on the ground. If he is not quick enough and "It" tags him, he must take "It's" place. If the day is cloudy, play *Tree Tag* instead. In this variation, a child is safe as long as he has his hand on a tree.

Pirates and Redskins

This game is a re-enactment of the exciting battle between Peter's friends, the Redskins, and his enemies, the fierce Pirates.

The two teams line up behind their boundary lines as shown in the diagram. Each has a prison, which is for captives. The territory between is "No Man's Land." One after the other, players venture

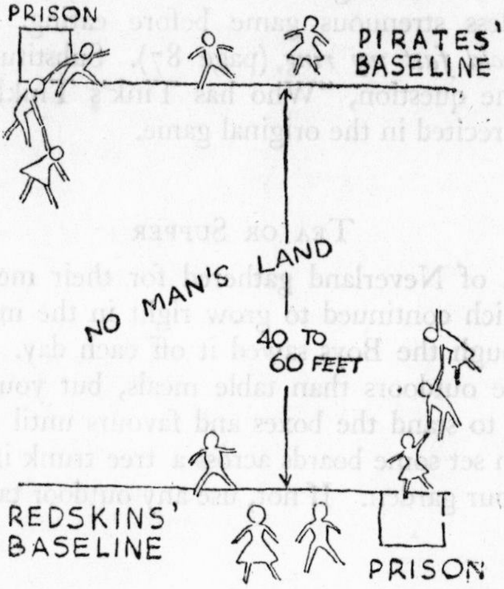

PRISON

PIRATES' BASELINE

NO MAN'S LAND

40 TO 60 FEET

REDSKINS' BASELINE

PRISON

into this area to try to tag players from the opposite side, or to make a successful run into enemy territory and back again. If a player gets across the enemy's base line and returns home safely, he is allowed to choose a prisoner from that side, or free a prisoner from his own team who is being held in the enemy camp.

A player may be tagged only by an opponent who leaves his base line after the player in question has left his. When a player is caught, he is put into prison. His team-mates can free him by touching his hand. He may reach as far out of the prison as possible, but must keep one foot on the line. When there are several prisoners, they may hold hands in single file and stretch toward their home line to make their release easier, but the last one must have his foot on the prison base. A guard should always be on hand to intercept rescuers. Only one prisoner may be freed at a time. On their way home a prisoner and his rescuer are free from being tagged.

This is a simplified version of *Prisoner's Base*, one of the most exciting and popular games for children. If your little friends are unacquainted with the rules, play the game once to make them clear and to settle any questions. When the children know the rules, you will have difficulty in calling a halt to this war between Pirates and Redskins.

Who has Tink's Tinkle Bell?

Wendy, who took such good care of the Boys, would undoubtedly recommend a less strenuous game before eating. Play the game *Biddy, Biddy, hold fast my ring* (page 87). Substitute a tiny bell for the ring, and the question, "Who has Tink's Tinkle Bell?" for the rhyme which is recited in the original game.

TEA OR SUPPER

The children of Neverland gathered for their meals round a tree-trunk table, which continued to grow right in the middle of Wendy's house, even though the Boys sawed it off each day. Box lunches are more practicable outdoors than table meals, but you will want some place on which to stand the boxes and favours until meal-time. Like Wendy, you can set some boards across a tree trunk if you have a flat-topped one in your garden. If not, use any outdoor table.

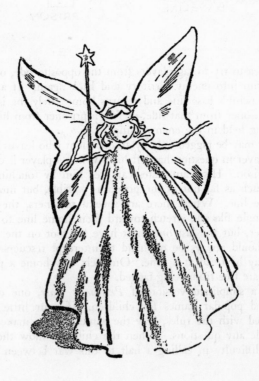

Tinker Bell would make a very pretty centrepiece. Make the figure like the larger Pierette doll described in Chapter 21. Dress Tink in foamy net or muslin. Give her yellow wool curls, a silver paper crown, tall, slender wings, and a star-tipped wand.

Serve the meal in boxes tied with white ribbon and decorated with tinkling bells. A good menu combination would be chicken and mayonnaise on white bread, and tomato and bacon in brown-bread sandwiches; iced cup cakes; bananas; and grape-fruit squash served in paper cups.

For favours, give each child a Peter Pan pipe or a toy bow and arrow set (the rubber-tipped kind), and one of these saucy Peter Pan hats.

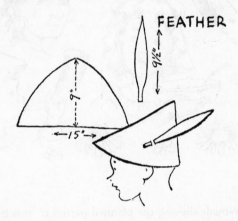

Make the hat of orange, and the feather of green kindergarten paper. Cut a double slit in one side of the hat through which to insert the feather.

After Supper

Before the children go home, let them live over again all the adventures of Peter and Wendy in the wonderful Neverland. Tell them about the J. M. Barrie Peter Pan Bequest. This means that Sir J. M. Barrie's royalties on all the versions of the Peter Pan story published by Messrs. Hodder & Stoughton, Ltd., go to help the doctors and nurses to cure children who are lying ill in the Great Ormond Street Hospital for Sick Children in London.

MAKE YOUR OWN PARTIES
13

LIKE ready-made dresses, the planned parties in this book may need a few tucks or alterations to fit particular requirements. But if you are one of those ingenious individuals who prefer to toss together original creations, you may find this scrapbag of ideas more to your liking. In it are thumb-nail sketches of some of the other themes which appeal to children under ten, as well as brief accounts of several successful parties.

MOTHER GOOSE PARTY

Mother Goose is always welcome at children's parties, for she brings in her train a host of characters who are as entertaining to meet in real life as between the pages of a book.

A Mother Goose party almost takes care of itself. Little children love dressing up as Bo-Peep, Mistress Mary, Jack Horner, or Tommy Tucker. Once in costume, their acting of the beloved jingles follows naturally. The rhymes suggest other games, too—a candlestick race,

a Miss Muffet Catching the Spider game, and a Mother Goose parade
to the table.

A doll dressed as Mistress Mary, with her watering-can, or as Bo-
Peep with her shepherd's crook, makes a charming centrepiece. A
Jack Horner Pie could never be more appropriate. Favours can be
Boy Blue horns, or lollipop maids with crêpe-paper bonnets tied under
their chins.

INDIAN PARTY

Give him a headband with a single feather, dab a little war paint on
his cheek, arm him with a toy bow and arrow, and your little warrior
will be off on the trail to fun and action. With whoops of enthusiasm,
the braves will compete in target contests, tag, and all kinds of scouting
and stalking games. A tomtom dance to finish off the pow-wow is
just about the greatest thrill imaginable to a just-pretend "Heap Big
Injun Chief."

If the party is held outdoors, erect a tepee and let the children make
up their own games and cook their own food over an open fire.

PETER RABBIT PARTY

This wonderful bunny cake provides a perfect excuse for a Peter
Rabbit Party.

The marshmallows are held together with cocktail sticks. Eyes, nose,
mouth, and buttons are drawn with one of the sticks dipped in red
vegetable colouring which has been diluted with water. The ears are

petal-shaped pieces of paper. Colour the inside with red crayon, and insert the ears into slits cut in the bunny heads.

Peter's weakness was Mr. McGregor's cabbage patch, but when he was not getting into mischief he was probably sunning himself in a daisy field. These gay little daisy stands would make attractive place-card holders. The centre is a yellow pastille, the stem a lollipop stick wrapped in green crêpe paper. The petals are cut from white kindergarten paper. Stand the flowers in miniature pots or in pastille holders.

What games would Peter play? *Hide and Seek* with Mr. McGregor, of course. And *Tag* when that cross-patch finds him. *Cat and Mouse*, described in the previous chapter, would be especially exciting if the children joined hands to form a circle-fence or briar patch, to protect Peter from Mr. McGregor, who was trying to break through from outside.

Step right in to see our Show!

When Peter and Brian were eight, they had so many friends to invite to their birthday party that they did not know how to entertain them. They were twins, you see, and that meant asking twice as many guests as most boys and girls have to their parties.

Peter finally had the bright idea. "Let's have a show!" he said. "Betty can do magic tricks and Bobby can bring his puppets." Betty and Bobbie were their older cousins. Brian thought a show would be great fun, so they planned it carefully.

The guests were not told immediately of the surprise in store. The first twenty minutes were spent undoing presents and testing the new toys and games. Then Peter asked everyone to be quiet, and announced that a show was going to be given in the next room.

The boys and girls were so excited that they wanted to rush in, pell-mell. But Peter explained that this was going to be a real show. Everyone was to receive a ticket. Brian would collect them at the door and show the boys and girls to their seats. The chairs were arranged in rows, and had big cards on the backs with numbers corresponding to those on the tickets.

The children loved this plan of Peter's. Although they could hardly control their enthusiasm, they entered the play-room-theatre as haughtily and as mannerly as first-night opera-goers.

The show lasted half an hour. Betty and Bobbie outdid themselves for the admiring audience. Tea followed the last curtain.

Peter and Brian and all their friends voted it the best party they had ever had.

A FAIRY WISHING WELL

Anne Morgan is the kind of little girl who looks for fairies in every blade of grass, in the stars at night, and even in the moon. For such a little girl a party would not be complete without her fairy friends.

Anne's fifth birthday party started in just the way most of her playmates' parties had begun. The children played circle games—*Mulberry Bush* and *Who has the Ring?*

They were still guessing *Who has left the Circle?* when Anne's father came in, and told them a story about fairies who had let their little friends who really-truly believed in them visit their fairy wishing well.

"Where is it?" Anne and her friends wanted to know right away. They believed in fairies. "Really! Truly!" "How do we get there?" "What do you have to do to find it?"

"Well, first you have to have fairy wings and crowns," Anne's father explained. "Then you have to follow the magic trail."

As if wishing had brought her there, Anne's mother appeared in the doorway with an armful of pink and blue crêpe-paper wings, and a box full of crowns. There was a great scramble. In a very few minutes, the wings were pinned to the children's backs, and tied to their wrists. The crowns were already put together, but each child decorated hers with stars and circles and bits of tinsel.

The fairy troop was clamouring to be off. Anne's father gave each one a string, which led to the other rooms, round chairs, under tables, and finally to—where do you suppose?—a wishing well in the centre of the tea table. Just as the children had expected, the good fairy had piled it high with gifts for her little friends.

ALICE-IN-WONDERLAND PARTY

Lewis Carroll's gay dream stories are bursting with party ideas for the children who know and love the winsome, long-haired Alice. Even the form of the invitation is suggested by Alice's idea of the mouse's "tale."

Come to our

House on

June the

Sixth at

Three-thir-

ty

to An

Alice

Etc.,

Etc.

Alice's looking-glass garden with its mass of flowers would make an entrancing centrepiece; or the chessmen might parade down the table past the grinning Cheshire cat; or else perch the Cat atop a Jack Horner Pie, decorated with cellophane ruffles and Heart playing-cards.

Humpty Dumpty eggs with pipe-cleaner legs make amusing favours. Sit them on paper cups filled with shredded paper and sweets.

The book suggests many ready-made games—a cactus race, where everybody wins, and Alice has to give each one a comfit; riddles asked by the March Hare; and croquet with live wickets. Of course you cannot play with hedgehogs and flamingoes, but some of the children could stoop with hands on the floor, to make arches, while the others crawl through in a race with another team.

What to eat? Alice has taken care of that also. "Some gave them white bread, some gave them brown; some gave them plum-cake——" We'll forget that they "drummed them out of town."

PIRATE PARTY

One of the most exciting adventures in the world to high-spirited six-to-ten-year-olds is to "play pirate," and swagger in the gaudy costumes and with the lusty manners of swashbuckling freebooters.

A Pirate Party can be very simple, or it can be in the grandiose manner. You can have a living-room party, and transform your young guests into buccaneers simply by tying red cambric bandanas on their heads, sashes round their waists, and metal curtain rings to their ears. You can also be a little bolder and have the party in the cellar, with kegs for seats, candles in bottles or tin cans replacing the electric lights, a table of packing-boxes covered with brown wrapping-paper, a parrot in a cage, and a skull-and-crossbones insignia over the doorway. The Jolly Roger is a "must" at all Pirate Parties.

Whatever else the pirates do, they sooner or later hunt for treasure. Cardboard field glasses or telescopes add to the fun of make-believe.

Party pirates will enjoy any other games with vigour and action. In choosing your programme, remember that pirates are a roaring, adventuresome, lusty lot of individuals.

Refreshments can be served picnic style at the table, or in individual boxes. Don't use glasses for the drinks. Pirates like to swill their potations from tin cups.

JACK HORNER PIES

The most popular centrepiece for children's-party tables takes its name from the Mother Goose boy who stuck in his thumb and pulled out a plum. The plums the children pull are the party favours, attached to ribbons which run from their plates to a gaily decorated box or deep baking dish, with a removable lid, placed in the centre of the table. A round hat box cut down several inches is best.

Cover the box and lid separately. Paste cellophane or crêpe-paper frills on the lid, and run a ribbon from it to the centre light, pulley-fashion. Lift the lid when the time comes for the children to pull the gifts from the Jack Horner pie.

Or cut holes in the box. Paste tissue paper over them and run the ribbons through narrow slits cut in the tissue. The gifts "pop" right out of the " windows " when the children pull their ribbon streamers.

MORE GAMES

14

FOR PARTIES AND PICNICS

THE first ten games are for children from four to six. Little children enjoy imitating their older brothers and sisters, and like to play grown-up games. If they do not seem to understand the rules, let them play the games the way they think they should be played. Have a prize for everyone—perhaps one colour for the winner and a different one for the loser. Once the children are in the game they are determined to receive a prize—that is, if prizes are being given. They can't see any justice in Johnny's getting a lollipop just because he crossed a line before they did. Johnny didn't work so hard, or he didn't scoop up the potatoes the way he was supposed to. Avoid tears and heartaches by refusing to see mistakes, and by rewarding participation, not winning.
• For additional games, consult the classified index.

TEN GAMES FOR FOURS TO SIXES
Orange Toss

From behind a throwing line, let the children toss oranges, potatoes, or rubber balls into baking-tins placed a short distance away.

Potato Race

Arrange two rows of three potatoes or oranges, placed equal distances apart. Let two children at a time run to the potatoes, pick them up and carry them to a box at the opposite end of the room. Five-year-olds can usually be made to pick up one potato at a time, and then run back for the others. Do not stress this point too much with four-year-olds.

Potato and Spoon Race

Have a race between two or three children. Each one carries a potato on a tablespoon. If the party is being held in the living-room, substitute coloured pebbles or wooden beads.

Ankle Race

The children bend over and grasp their ankles with their hands. In this position they waddle a distance of 20 ft. to a finishing line.

Lollipop Race

Place a row of lollipops along the finish line ten feet from the starting tape. There should be one less than the number of players. Blow a whistle as a signal that the race is on. The child who does not get a lollipop is eliminated from the game. Give him a lollipop as a consolation prize, but collect the lollipops from the other children and arrange them as before. Continue until only two runners remain. Award a box of lollipops or some other inexpensive prize to the boy or girl who wins this heat. The game requires too much time and concentration for an indoor programme, but is an excellent choice for picnics.

Balloon Push

Provide each child with a balloon of a distinctive colour. Simultaneously, the competitors start batting the balloons gently across the room to a finish line. The first one to get his across wins the game. Balloons seldom follow a straight course, so don't be surprised if the players get into a few tangles. That's the reason for the different colours.

Flag Race

Stick flags into six potatoes. Place them as you would for a potato race, three in a row in two parallel lines. Two children at a time race to bring back the nearest, then the middle, then the farthest flag and holder.

Broomstick Ride

Astride toy broomsticks, two or three players engage in a galloping horse race. When the first race ends, three fresh horses compete.

Charlie Over the Water

Charlie stands in the centre of the circle while the other children walk round him, chanting the following rhyme:

> Charlie over the water,
> Charlie over the sea,
> Charlie caught a big fish
> But can't catch me.

On the last word, the children squat quickly. If Charlie can tag a player before he stoops, Charlie joins the circle, and the other child takes his place in the centre.

Jack, be Nimble

Place two or three unlighted candles in a row. Each child in turn jumps over them while the others recite the rhyme:

> Jack, be nimble,
> Jack, be quick,
> Jack, jump over the candlestick.

SINGING GAMES

Indoors or outdoors, singing games have an endless fascination. Some old favourites such as Oranges and Lemons, Nuts in May, Poor Jenny is a-weeping, are too well known to need description, but the games given here may prove useful alternatives. All are old, time-tested song-dramatizations. Their origins are buried in the misty past. Yet children of to-day play them for hours on end, just as their grandmothers did long years ago.

Go round and round the Village

This is one of the best loved of singing games. The game starts with one player walking round the outside of the circle formed by the other children. He continues "going round the village" during the first verse. On the second, the children in the circle raise their joined hands and the little traveller weaves in and out underneath them, while all the children sing:

Go in and out the window, etc.

During the third verse the circle players stoop down, and the other child steps in and out over the doorsteps to the words:

Go in and out the doorsteps, etc.

The fourth verse is self-explanatory:

Go kneel before a partner, etc.

Both children bow in farewell to the circle players during the next verse:

One bow before we leave you, etc.

Both children now "go round the village." The game is repeated until too few children remain in the circle to form the doorsteps and windows. One of these players is chosen to start the game from the beginning, or to be "It" in a new game.

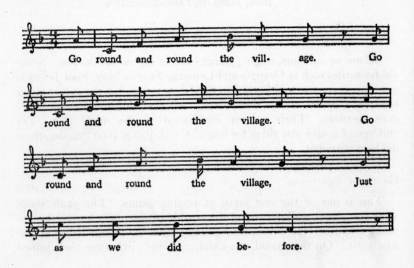

London Bridge

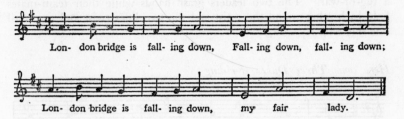

Lon- don bridge is fall- ing down, Fall- ing down, fall- ing down;

Lon- don bridge is fall- ing down, my fair lady.

London Bridge is falling down, falling down, falling down;
London Bridge is falling down, my fair lady.
  Build it up with iron bars, etc.
Iron bars will rust away, etc.
  Build it up with pins and needles, etc.
Pins and needles rust and bend, etc.
  Build it up with gold and silver, etc.
Gold and silver will be stolen away, etc.
  Here's a prisoner I have got, etc.
What's the prisoner done to you? etc.
  Stole my watch and broke my crown, etc.
What will you take to set him free? etc.
  One hundred pounds will set him free, etc.
One hundred pounds I have not got, etc.
  Then off to prison he must go, etc.

Two children join hands and hold them high to form a bridge. The others form a line by placing their hands on the shoulders of the boy or girl in front of them. The procession circles round and under the arch while the children sing the song. At each repetition of the phrase "My fair lady," the bridge falls down. If the player is captured, he leaves the line of marchers and places his hands on the shoulders of one of the two players forming the arch. When the players are under six or seven, the last player to be captured wins the game.

Older children add a fanciful touch and a tug of war at the end. Before the game starts the two bridge players choose an extravagant object with which to ensnare the captive. When a prisoner is taken, he is asked quietly, "Would you like a golden horse or silver wings?" or whatever objects they have chosen. If the captive says that he would like a golden horse, he stands behind whichever player selected the horse.

C.P.—6

When all the players have been taken prisoner, the two sides have a tug-of-war. The two leaders grasp hands while their team-mates hold each other round the waist and the two lines twist and tug until one side wins.

Here come Three Dukes A-riding

Here come three dukes a-riding, a-riding, a-riding.
Here come three dukes a-riding, o-aye-o!

What are you riding here for? etc.
We're riding here to get married, etc.

Marry one of us, sirs, etc.
You're all too black and dirty, etc.
We're good enough for you, sirs, etc.
You're all as stiff as pokers, etc.
We can bend as well as you, sirs, etc.

Thro' the kitchen and thro' the hall
I choose the fairest of you all.
The fairest one that I can see
Is pretty Miss ——, walk with me.

Three dukes come courting a line of "sassy" maids. The dukes approach and retreat from the line in which the other players are standing, while the three of them sing the first verse. Then they stand still, and the maids walk towards the dukes and away from them and sing the second verse. The game continues with the questions and answers going back and forth until the last verse, when the dukes choose one of the fair ladies.

Strangely enough, the maid changes her sex immediately, and then four dukes come a-riding. But children do not quibble about such details. The game is repeated until all the children have joined the dukes.

Itiskit, Itaskit

To many children this game is better known as *I sent a Letter to my Love*. One of the children is given a handkerchief. While the others sing, she walks round the outside of the circle, drops the kerchief behind one of the players and then races back to her own place. When the child to whom she sent her "letter" discovers the handkerchief, she picks it up, chases the child who dropped it, and tries to tag her before the latter reaches "home." If she is successful, the first child must take the handkerchief and go round the circle once more. If not, the child who received the "letter" walks round the circle and drops the kerchief while the children repeat the song.

I- tis- kit, I- tas- kit, a green and yell- ow bas- ket. I sent a let- ter to my love and on the way he dropped it. Drip, drop the hand- ker- chief. Drip, drop the handkerchief. Drip, drop the handker- chief to the one that you love best.

A-hunting We Will Go

Unlike the majority of singing games, this is played in two parallel lines rather than in a circle. The two leaders join hands and slide up and down between the lines until the word "go" at the end of the song. Then they drop hands quickly, run to the head of their own line, round the outside, and take their places at the foot. The first one to get into position scores a point for his side. The singing, sliding, and racing continue until each has had a turn. Points are totalled and the team that has scored most wins the game.

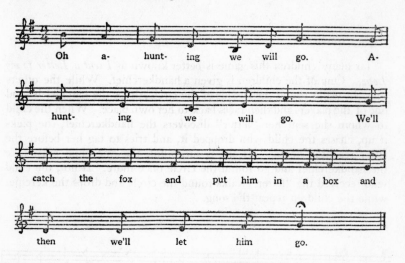

Oh a- hunt- ing we will go. A-
hunt- ing we will go. We'll
catch the fox and put him in a box and
then we'll let him go.

Did you ever see a Lassie?

Did you ever see a lassie, a lassie, a lassie,
Did you ever see a lassie go this way and that?

Go this way and that way, go this way and that way,
Did you ever see a lassie go this way and that?

One child stands in the centre of the ring. The others join hands and walk round him singing the words to the tune, *Ach du Lieber Augustin*. When the phrase "Go this way and that way" is reached the first time, the child in the centre jumps up and down, claps his hands over his head, or performs some other action. The circle players imitate him, and continue their performance during the remainder of the song.

Then the child in the centre rejoins the circle, and chooses another to take his place in the centre.

INDOOR GAMES

Simon Says (also called O'Grady Says)

Choose one of the players to play the part of Simon. He stands in the centre of the circle issuing rapid-fire orders, which the others must obey only if they are preceded by the words, "Simon says."

He may say, "Stand up, Bobby!" Bobby doesn't move. But if the boy in the centre calls out, "Simon says, 'Stand up, Bobby,'" then Bobby must rise immediately, or take Simon's place.

Simon can request the players to perform all kinds of actions—stand up, sit down, turn round, stand on their heads, do a somersault, chatter like a monkey, or fly like a bird.

Hot Beans

This is a variation of the well-known *Hunt the Thimble*. One child leaves the room while the others hide a specified object. When they are ready, they call "It" back with the following rhyme:

> Hot beans and melted butter!
> Please, my lady, come to supper.

When "It" comes near to the hidden object the group calls out, "Hot beans." When he draws away, they say, "Cold beans." After the object has been found, "It" chooses another child to take his place.

As a variation, let all the children but one leave the room while "It" hides the object.

Clap In, Clap Out

As in the previous game, one child leaves the room, while the others hide an object or decide on some action which "It" must perform on his return. When "It" comes back to the room this time, he may ask the question, "Is it something to find or to do?" Guided by the reply, "It" searches for the object or tries to discover what performance is expected of him. The other players help him by clapping when he "gets warm" and stamping when he is "off the track."

Let each child have a turn. The game is won by the child who takes the shortest time to execute the required performance.

Hunt the Slipper

A slipper is passed from hand to hand outside a circle. Occasionally one of the players taps it on the floor to taunt "It," who is inside, and is trying to catch one of them with the slipper in his hand. Anyone caught takes "It's" place.

Animal Guessing Game

Whisper to each child the name of an animal. When called on, the child mentions three facts about the quadruped assigned to him, and the others try to identify it. The first one to name the animal wins a point.

Which Instrument is it?

While one of the players pretends to play a musical instrument, the others try to guess what it is. The one who does so has the next turn to mime a musical performance. The game sounds too simple to be much fun, but it is a great favourite.

Telephone

Players stand or sit in a line. The leader, or one of the children, whispers a nonsensical message to the first player. He relays it to the second, the second to the third, and so on down the line. When the message reaches the last player, he repeats it aloud, and the leader tells what the message should have been. Usually there is little resemblance between them, especially when the original was some such silly jingle as:

> Fuzzy wuzzy was a bear.
> Fuzzy wuzzy had no hair.

Pussy wants a Corner

As you will probably remember, each child has a corner or base, except Pussy. Poor, homeless Pussy approaches each of the children and says, "Pussy wants a corner." But they don't want him, and they reply, "Next-door neighbour." Pussy tries the next one. When he isn't looking, the other players try to exchange places. If Pussy can reach one of the vacant corners, the player whom he has displaced must take Pussy's place and go begging for a home.

Biddy, Biddy, hold fast my Ring

The players sit in a circle with their hands extended and their palms together, as if they were praying. The child in the centre holds his hands in the same way, but conceals a ring between them. When everyone is ready, he walks round the circle and slides his closed hands between each player's palms while he recites this verse:

> Biddy, Biddy, hold fast my gold ring,
> Till I go to London and come back again.

He secretly slips the ring into the hands of one of the players, but continues round the circle and repeats the ritual and the rhyme for each player, so that the others do not know in whose possession he has left the ring.

After "It" has completed the circuit, each child in turn tries to guess who has the ring. The first one to do so takes the place of the child in the centre. If none of the guesses is correct, "It" has another turn to hide the ring.

Here I Brew

One child is chosen to be the "captive." The others form a circle round him. The "captive" tries to break out of the circle by force and strategy. Walking inside, he touches one pair of joined hands and says, "Here I brew." Then he touches a second pair and says, "Here I bake." The third time he is especially cautious. He strolls casually, and when the players are least expecting it, he wheels around and tries to break through a third pair of joined hands. As he does so, he shouts, "Here I bake my wedding cake." If he succeeds in getting through, the player on the right of the space through which he made his break takes his place. If he is not able to escape, he is "It" once more.

O'Clock

The players sit in a single row. Two are chosen to step aside and choose a number from one to twelve. When they return, they ask the other players in turn, "What o'clock is it?" Each one guesses and the one who mentions the right time has a chance to choose between two objects which the players who asked the questions now select for themselves. The objects are usually extravagant flights of fancy. Most of the time the questions take such form as, "Would you rather have a golden chariot or a silver crown?" "Would you rather have an aeroplane or a motor-cycle?"

If the player who guessed the correct time chooses the motor-cycle, he goes out with the player who selected the object. The other joins the players in a line, and takes his turn at guessing the next "o'clock."

OUTDOOR GAMES

Twelve O'Clock

A sly old fox sits by a tree or in some other shady spot. The other players are chickens. They know where the fox is, and to protect the brood the players hold each other round the waist and walk in a single line.

The chickens have one bad failing. They are curious about the time. Every few seconds they approach the Fox and say, "Please, Mr. Fox, what time is it?" If he says, one o'clock, five o'clock, or even twelve *nooooon*, the chickens may walk away in peace. But midnight is the dangerous hour, and if the Fox replies, "Twelve midnight," the chickens scramble for safety behind their own line. Any straggler who gets caught exchanges places with the fox.

Hill Dill

Draw two boundary lines about thirty feet apart. "It" stands between the two lines. The other players stand behind one of them. When "It" shouts, "Hill Dill come over the hill, or else I'll catch you standing still," the players attempt to cross to the opposite boundary line. Any players caught remain with "It" and help him capture the others.

To vary the game, "It" can call the names of individual players instead of the whole group.

Red Rover

This game is played like Hill Dill, except that "It" calls individuals with the following rhyme:

> Red Rover, Red Rover,
> Let (*player's name*) come over.

Statues

This game is played in couples by any number of children. Partners grasp right hands and whirl each other round and round while the leader or one of the children calls out, "Faster, Faster." When the leader shouts, "Let go," the players "freeze." The leader then asks each statue, "What are you?" Answers are as ludicrous as the poses, but anyone who laughs or moves while the leader is making his rounds of the gallery is eliminated or pays a forfeit.

Occupation

Children never seem to tire of this traditional game with its silly jingle. Two teams are formed. The group that is chosen to start goes some distance away from the other team and chooses a trade or occupation. Then they approach the second team and, in a chorus, engage in the following dialogue:

> FIRST TEAM: "Here we come."
> SECOND TEAM: "Where from?"
> FIRST TEAM: "The West Countree."
> SECOND TEAM: "What's your number?"
> FIRST TEAM: "Cucumber."
> SECOND TEAM: "What's your trade?"
> FIRST TEAM: "Lemonade."
> SECOND TEAM: "Show us some or you won't get paid."

The first team mentions the first letter or letters of the words which describe their trade, and then start miming the action. Their occupation might be: "P. C."—picking cherries; "S. B."—sewing buttons; "M. S."—mending shoes. The first child to guess the trade scores a point. The second team then has a turn at choosing an occupation.

The game is often played with tagging and chasing at the end. When it is, the first team approaches the second in a line, with hands joined. As soon as one of the children on the opposite side mentions the correct word or words, the first team dashes for safety to a line about 20 ft. away. The players of the second team pursue them, and any players they tag must join their side. Then they choose a trade, which the first team tries to guess. The team which has most players at the close of the playing time wins the game.

Where was Bobby standing Before?

One child is "It." He holds his hands over his eyes or is blind-folded, while children in the circle change places. The blindfold is removed, and the leader says, "Where was Bobby standing before?" The leader names a particular child. "It" has two chances to guess. If he does not succeed, he must let the child referred to take his place.

PART II

JOLLY PARTIES FOR THE EARLY 'TEENS

THE parties in the first section are for younger children. This section contains a variety of do-it-yourself parties—the kind you and your friends can plan together.

Party-planning is as much fun as party-giving. Learning how to arrange an attractive table, how to offer appetizing menus and novel entertainments—in short, learning how to become a good host or hostess is all a part of growing up.

Try the parties and games suggested here. Adapt and develop them to suit your own ideas and requirements.

A HALLOWE'EN PARTY

15

FOR OLDER CHILDREN

NOW that you and your friends are old enough to laugh at Hallowe'en and its ghosts, plan a real Hallowe'en party, with its accompanying witches and black cats.

Send your invitations on orange-coloured paper, in the following rhyme:

> *Put on your mask and costume,*
> *Come early, don't be late,*
> *If at our Witches' Gambol*
> *You'd choose to learn your fate.*

Decorate the room with cut-outs of bats, cats, and the usual trappings. Small witches could be hung round the walls. These are easily made from coat-hangers with witches' masks fastened to the hooks and black material hung over the hangers to suggest witches' drapery. White gloves can be added to the ends of the hangers.

To give additional Hallowe'en atmosphere, one of your friends whose voice is easily recognisable might dress up as a comic ghost and entertain the children with some tricks.   Many stunts will suggest themselves, but avoid anything eerie or unpleasant.

You have promised your guests that they will learn their fate at the party, so don't disappoint them.   Begin the fun with some of the traditional fortune games.   They are always fascinating to children who are just beginning to accumulate their own store of Hallowe'en lore. Moreover, they are perfect party-openers, and late-comers can be included as they arrive.

Fortune Games

Wheel of Fortune

Suspend a hoop from the ceiling on a single cord or wire so that the hoop can be rotated.   Attach strings, and tie or glue to each string one of the following objects:

Object	Fortune
Ring	Happy marriage
Thimble	Life of single blessedness
Sixpence	Rich man
Farthing	Poor man
Needle and thread	Tailor
Roll of adhesive plaster	Doctor
Note-book	Lawyer
Tiny basket	Merchant
Tin soldier	General
Boat	Admiral

Blindfold each child in turn, give him a pair of blunt scissors, and lead him to the hoop.   Then give it a spin and let the child snip his fate from the whirling wheel of fortune.   Have replacements for any of the objects cut down.

Apple-paring Fortune

One of the oldest Hallowe'en superstitions is the belief that an apple peel thrown over the left shoulder will reveal the initial of the mate-to-be.   If the paring breaks or does not form a letter, marriage is not to be the thrower's fortune.

GROUP GAMES

Bubble, Bubble, Toil and Trouble

With the menacing words of her Macbeth sisters, the witch in this game tries to ensnare her victims. It is not nearly so "scary" as it sounds. The words are added only to give a little Hallowe'en zip to an old party favourite.

Players are seated in a circle. The one who is chosen to be "The Witch" walks around inside. Without warning, she stops in front of one of the players, points her finger and says very quickly, "Right—Bubble, bubble, toil and trouble." Before she can finish the phrase, the player to whom the witch pointed must give the full name of the player on his right. If the witch says, "Left—Bubble, bubble, toil and trouble," the player must give the name of the boy or girl seated to his left. If he fails, he must take the witch's place.

Making the players change seats occasionally "keeps them on their toes" and makes the game more exciting.

Get Rid of the Witch

This game is played in the same formation as the previous one. The players rapidly pass a bean bag made of black cloth in the shape of a witch's head. Facial features are sewn or painted on the cloth. The object of the game is to get rid of the bean bag before the leader blows a whistle or rings a bell. The leader should have her back to the players and sound the signal at unexpected intervals.

Any player caught with the bean bag pays a penalty. The first time he must rest his arm on his head and keep it there. The second time he extends one leg; the third time, both legs. He must remain in this position and pass the bean bag with only one hand. The fourth time he is caught he is eliminated from the game.

Sardines

If the house is large and can stand up to rough treatment, dim the lights and play this slightly rough-house game of hide-and-seek. One player hides while the others have their eyes covered. When he is safely hidden, the rest search for him. Instead of revealing his hiding-place, the players who find him crawl in with him. The last one to find the others is "It" the next time.

Witches' Clatter

Cats miaow, dogs bark, ghosts groan, and witches hiss in this rattle-clatter game.

Arrange the players in four groups—cats, dogs, ghosts, and witches. Appoint a leader for each one. Individually or in groups, the players search for Hallowe'en cut-outs which you have previously hidden round the house. Anyone may uncover a cut-out, but only the leaders may pick it up. To attract the attention of the leader, a player who finds one must groan if he is a ghost, bark if he is a dog, miaow if he is a cat, and hiss if he is a witch. When four or five players begin howling at once, you can imagine what a din and clatter there is going to be.

As soon as a leader hears a signal, he rushes to pick up the cut-out before one of the other leaders can get there. The group that retrieves the largest number wins the game.

Actor Antics

With everyone in costume, why not put on a show? Not just an ordinary show, but one which tests the wits and ingenuity of actors and audience alike.

Keep intact the teams from the previous game, and send each to a different corner of the room. These are the four separate casts which are going to present competitive performances. Provide each with a pile of newspapers, a paper of pins, and some lengths of cloth or drapery to create the props and costume changes, or the accessories their acts may require.

Announce quietly to the four groups the dramatization they are to prepare and present within five minutes. It may be some amusing incident which is known to the company. It might be an historical episode such as supposedly took place between Queen Elizabeth and Raleigh; or a scene from a popular film, comic strip, or book.

The groups may perform the act you suggest, or may choose one of their own. Leaders draw numbers to see which cast presents its performance first. While one group is acting, the others try to guess the title or subject of their dramatization. Award inexpensive prizes to the group that gives the best performance and to the one whose subject is hardest to guess.

Although you may not think of your friends as film stars, we'll wager that some of the comedies you see in this game will rival Hollywood at its best.

Serial Story

Players sit in a circle, and one starts the game by telling an impromptu story. At an exciting point he breaks off the tale, and his right-hand neighbour takes it up, making of it what he fancies. Thus the tale goes round the circle, gathering thrills and absurdities at an amazing rate, and working up to an incredible climax or anti-climax.

APPLE-DUCKING

To make the party complete, you must include this traditional sport, for which the entire company had better troop into the kitchen or some other suitable place.

The game consists in trying to catch floating apples with a fork dropped from the teeth. The apples should be kept bobbing about in a tub of water—an occasional stir keeps them lively. From over a chair-back, each player takes a turn at "ducking," i.e. aiming at a bobbing apple with a fork held between the teeth, and at the right moment letting the fork drop on it. Not so easy as it seems! Successful "duckers" keep their apples.

TIME FOR REFRESHMENTS

Paint some black crescent moons on a large oblong of orange-coloured paper. Make this the centrepiece on which to place the Witch-in-Chief.

For small witches which stand at each child's place, use round lollipops on 4-in. sticks. Cover the cellophane-wrapped sweet with peach crêpe paper. Affix green semicircles for eyes, and a red slit for a mouth. These can be cut from gummed dots or seals. Glue straggly red wool hair on the back and top of the head.

Insert the lollipop stick in a $1\frac{1}{2}$-in. button mould. Bend a single pipe cleaner round the top of the stick to form arms. Make the dress of black crêpe paper. Gather round the neck and smooth the ruffle back from the face to conceal the string. Cut slits for armholes and pull through these the ends of the pipe cleaners.

Gather yellow wool round the middle of a 3-in. cocktail stick to make a broom. The crown of the hat is a cone of black kindergarten paper, made from a $1\frac{1}{4}$-in. semicircle and pasted together. The brim is a $2\frac{1}{2}$-in. circle. Fix the brim to the crown by cutting a $\frac{1}{4}$-in. circle from the centre of the brim and making $\frac{1}{4}$-in. notches round the inside edge. Fold back the tabs and paste to crown.

The witch in the centre is a larger duplicate, fashioned in the same way, except that a pastille is used for the face and a 10-in. wire for the body. Use a strong wire; double it if necessary. The other measure-

ments are as follows: Hat, 3¼ in. semicircle for the crown, 4½-in. circle for the brim; 2-in. button mould base; 10-in. broomstick.

Perch the Witch-in-Chief astride her broomstick on top of a cauldron filled with gaily-coloured crackers. Any suitably-sized bowl, covered with black crêpe paper, will make a good cauldron.

SUPPER MENU

Assorted sandwiches   *Small sausages on sticks*
Orange iced layer cake
Trifle   *Fruit Delight*
Ice cream   *Chocolate biscuits*
Tea   *Cocoa*   *Lemonade*   *Apples*   *Nuts*

(Recipe for *Fruit Delight* on page 156.)

Have a plentiful supply of fruit drinks and glasses available throughout the evening, so that your guests may help themselves when thirsty.

16

A Family Christmas Party

CHRISTMAS is the season of the year when the family, however scattered, makes strenuous efforts to meet again round the festive table. You probably have had great joy in choosing or making appropriate gifts, and in thinking out unique and original ways of wrapping them into attractive packages. That has been your part in getting ready for Christmas.

At home, mother has put in some busy days of preparation, to ensure that all the family, with perhaps a few intimate guests, may enjoy the traditional fare which she has prepared with such care and enthusiasm. On Christmas Day she generally does the officiating, and by the time the meal is over, she is often too tired to think out bright and novel ways of amusing her guests.

Now this is where you can step in. Why not offer to make the decorating of the Christmas table and the entertaining of the party your entire responsibility?

TABLE DECORATIONS

Holly and mistletoe are already all round the house, and flowers at this time of year are difficult and expensive. The following centrepiece is a departure from the usual, and is most effective.

Arrange a few tall red candles in flat holders round a bed of evergreens, which you have liberally besprinkled with scarlet berries of any kind; or, if you are having dessert, you can use a tastefully arranged bowl of fruit and nuts as the centre. The bowl could be made from a hollowed-out half of a big golden pumpkin, its edges being scalloped with a sharp knife. The gay candles can be ranged round the bowl. (The candles are very effective unlit, if candlelight is not desired.)

At each place put an orange basket, which you can make the previous day. Cut thick-skinned oranges in half. Scoop out the pulp (which can be used for fruit salad), and with a sharp knife scallop the edges of each half. For each basket make a square-shaped handle of two pipe cleaners, inserting the ends through the basket as shown in sketch. Along the top of the handle fix a tiny, gaily-coloured cracker, with a name card attached. The pipe cleaners may be concealed by twisting round them bright green and scarlet ribbons.

Fill the little baskets with raisins and salted almonds (for recipe see page 156), and you have seasonable and gay little favours made with little trouble.

Some Games to Play

No one feels like putting forth any great exertion after a Christmas dinner, but often the mood is just right for a friendly easy-going guessing game.

Coffee Pot

This is a very good choice for such an occasion.

One player leaves the room while the others select an action verb for him to guess on his return. Such words as dress, comb, sleep, bath, and eat, which are concerned with every-day activities, are best if the ages are mixed and younger children and adults are playing together.

When "It" returns, he asks questions in which the words *Coffee Pot* are substituted for the missing verb. Questions must be worded so that they can be answered by "Yes" or "No." "It" might say to Mother, for example, "Did you *coffee pot* within the last hour?" The word chosen is "sleep" and Mother's reply is a very definite "No." To six-year-old David, who is the family sleepy-head, he asks, "Do you like to *coffee pot*?" Everyone is highly amused when David, with a sheepish grin, reluctantly answers, "Yes."

After you have played the game several times, you can include words which are not so common as those given above. Questions need not be asked of each player in turn, but the same person may not be interrogated twice in succession. The one whose reply reveals the chosen word takes "It's" place.

Cahoots

Here's a game which will keep your friends guessing for hours. If they don't guess the trick within five or ten minutes, play some other games and then come back to this one now and again, teasing them with it just when they are beginning to relax.

You will need a confederate—and who would be better than your mother? Start the game by saying to her, "Are you in cahoots with me?" If she answers, "Yes," continue with the following questions: "Do you feel as I feel?" "Do you see as I see?" If her answers are all in the affirmative, say to her, "Then close your eyes and tell me at whom I am pointing." Mother dutifully obeys and promptly gives the name of the right person. The guests are duly mystified. They beg you to repeat the statements so that they can watch you and your mother for signals. Of course you oblige, but still they do not seem to guess the trick. Finally they send your mother into the next room. Still she can name the person at whom you point.

How do you manage this wonderful thought-reading trick? Simply by agreeing with your mother that the person to whom you will point will be the last person who spoke before you asked, "Are you in cahoots with me?" If several people break into the conversation, so that she is not sure whom you have in mind, she simply answers, "No." Then you wait until the chattering subsides a little, and ask the question later.

Cahoots is, without doubt, one of the best of the "trick" party games. Play it once and you will certainly join the ranks of the enthusiasts.

Similarities

This brand-new treasure hunt is one the whole family will enjoy. There are no complicated clues to work out. All you have to do is to assemble a collection of common, every-day items and place them on or near objects in the room which are of similar colour. That is where the game gets its name and, incidentally, makes an object in plain sight as hard to find as a needle in a haystack.

Put a penny on a dark table, or on the base of a bronze lamp; a thimble on a chromium or silver ash tray; a gold safety-pin or collar button on a yellow chair, cushion, or curtain; a paper clip on a lamp shade of light colour; a red eraser next to a book or magazine with a red cover; a white pin or pearl cuff-links on a white table cloth; a piece of brown-wrapped toffee on the staircase; and a dark pencil on the window sill.

Conceal the objects while no one is in the room. Be sure that no duplicates are lying around. Extra clips or pencils, for instance, would confuse the searchers.

Prepare for each person a list of the hidden items. When you are ready to play the game, distribute the lists and explain that players are to search individually, and to write on their lists the position of any objects they find. All must be careful not to reveal the hiding-place to the other players, and nobody is allowed to touch any of the objects. Also explain that nothing in the room need be moved.

The players will start off gaily, sure of finding the objects within two minutes. But, as if by magic, they have melted into the background. Soon you will be deluged with questions. "Are you sure you don't have to move anything?" "Did you say all of them are in this room?" Before the game ends, everyone will be searching with the determination of the pioneers in the Gold Rush.

Santa Claus Artists

Provide pencils and paper for the players. Ask each one to draw a 2-in. square on his sheet and scatter fifteen dots inside it at random. Now tell them to connect the dots to make a Santa Claus face.

As you can guess, the results will be anything but artistic. Here's the only face I could draw with my fifteen dots. The additional lines added for effect on the beard and tassel are within the rules of the game.

The essential outlines of the drawing, however, must pass through the dots. Award small prizes for the most realistic and for the funniest faces.

CARD GAMES

Certain types of card games which are entirely fun, and which do not require particular skill, are among the best games for children and adults to play together. Father's longer reach does not help him as it does in tennis, and Mother's quick answers which always make her champion in guessing games do not bring her the winning cards. Competition is more even than in many athletic and social games. Chance favours everyone alike. Eight-year-old Hugh is just as likely to win as Aunt Elizabeth.

Two particularly good games in this category are *Pig* and *I Doubt It*.

Pig

Although any number can play, the game is best with from five to thirteen players. Take from the pack a set of four cards for each player. Any set will do—four Eights, four Tens, etc. Shuffle the cards and deal them one at a time. Players may not pick up their cards until the dealer gives the signal. The object of the game is to secure one of the sets of four matching cards.

As soon as the players have had an opportunity of looking at their cards and of deciding which one to discard, the dealer says, "Pass." Simultaneously, everyone passes a card along the table, face down, to his right-hand neighbour. If a player decides to keep the card he receives, he discards another from his hand. Cards are passed again as soon as the dealer gives the signals. These should be snappy, and the passing in quick tempo. The game continues until one of the players receives four cards of a kind.

Then the riot starts. In the centre of the table is a pile of match sticks, counters, or pennies, one less than the number of players. The moment a player collects a set of four matching cards, he grabs one of the pennies or other counters. As soon as he reaches towards the centre of the table, the other players grab too, whether or not they are also holding four cards of a kind. The player who is left without a counter becomes a third of a "Pig." Then a second round starts, and the cards are shuffled and dealt by the person to the right of the dealer.

When a player becomes a whole "Pig," a set of cards and one of the counters are removed and he is eliminated from the passing—but not from the game. He remains at the table, heckles the other players, and tries to trap them into talking to him. Anyone who speaks to a "Pig" becomes a third of a "Pig" himself. If he is already two-thirds, he becomes a whole "Pig" and is also eliminated from the passing.

Excitement runs high when the "Pigs" begin to badger the remaining players with tantalizing questions and remarks which are difficult to ignore.

I Doubt it

Any number can play. When there are more than thirteen, however, have two games at different tables. For more than six players, use two packs of cards.

Shuffle and deal the cards, one at a time, until they have all been distributed. Deal all the cards, even though some players may receive an extra one.

The person to the right of the dealer starts the game by placing any number of Aces face down on the table. He does not have to show the cards, but must call them Aces, regardless of what he plays. He must also announce the number he is playing. Remember that there are four Aces when you are using one pack of cards, and eight when you are using two.

Suppose that this first player does not have a single Ace in his hand. Does he admit it? He does not. He bluffs, and puts down as many cards as he thinks he can get rid of safely. If no one challenges him, the cards remain in the centre of the table and the next person plays in turn.

This player has to put down Two's. Perhaps he is feeling a bit cocky. Not having a single Two in his hand, he discards a Queen, a Jack, an Ace, and a Ten and nonchalantly announces, "Four Two's." But one of the players is suspicious and says, "I doubt it!" Anyone can challenge at any time, and the player doubted must show his cards. In this instance, if the second player had really put down four Two's, as he announced, the challenger would have to take all the cards on the table. Since the player who was doubted did not discard Two's, he takes back his own cards, plus those disposed of by the preceding player or players.

The object of the game, as you have probably guessed, is to get rid of one's cards. But that is not always easy when the cards must be played in order. What happens when a player is holding only Tens and he is supposed to play a Queen? Can he be truthful and skip his turn? Unfortunately for him, players must prevaricate in this game and play every time their turn comes round, and when a person is doubted and he has not played the right card, he must pick up the discard, whether it contains two cards or fifty.

Cards are won and lost at a furious pace. But eventually, in spite of all the doubting, someone manages to get rid of his entire hand. He wins the game and the dubious honour of being the best prevaricator in the family.

In the Hat

A pleasant game which requires little energy but which can become an exciting contest is *Card Tossing*, also called *In the Hat*. The competing player sits in a chair and tosses a pack of playing cards, one at a time, into a hat 5 ft. away. Play a second or third round if the players are determined to outdo each other.

AFTER SUPPER

Surely there can be no better finish to a family Christmas party than a few well-known carols, in which young and old can join, and some old-fashioned songs.

for
Christmas
Eve

17

A GOOD NEIGHBOURS' PARTY

SO much joy comes to us at Christmas that it is an added happiness to radiate its gaiety and goodwill to others less fortunate than ourselves.

There are so many ways in which we can do this. A Christmas party that I remember very happily from my youth was one at which we made Christmas stockings for a nearby orphanage. The stockings were made of strong red net, and were of generous size. We filled them with inexpensive toys, apples, oranges, nuts, and home-made sweets. When the last stocking was filled, we had our own party, enjoying it the more because we had worked for other children.

Some young friends of mine spent happy hours making a toy village to go under the Christmas tree in a day nursery. The houses, made from cardboard boxes, were gaily painted, had cellophane windows, and the roofs were given the seasonable sparkle by some Christmas frost sprinkled over gum.

Boys can have great fun repairing and repainting the toys they have outgrown and discarded.

A Christmas play or variety show might be presented, and the proceeds given to some local charity.

Perhaps the simplest, and certainly the most traditional way, is to organize a carol party. Plan your singing where carols would be most appreciated, e.g. at an Old People's Home, or somewhere where you know people might be lonely and neglected; and arrange your singing visit for the early part of the evening.

After one of these practical ways of wishing others a "Merry Christmas," gather your co-workers at your house for some fun and games for yourselves.

MORE GAMES FOR CHRISTMAS PARTIES

What Day is Christmas?

This is a jovial game which can be played throughout the party. Give each player a piece of cardboard on which to write his name, and a pin to fasten it to his coat or to her dress. The object of the game is to collect name tags. Anyone who can get another person to tell him on what day Christmas falls wins that player's card. The boy or girl who loses it may try to get it back by trapping the questioner when he is thinking of something else; or he can approach some other victim. The question can be asked in any way. You may say to your best friend, "Oh, I forgot to get a present for Aunt Gertrude. Are the shops open on Friday?" If she is helpful and says, "No, that's Christmas," you win her tag. Or you can try a simpler question: "Is Christmas on Thursday or Friday?" If you get the right answer, you collect a name tag. The game starts off slowly, but its hilarity will increase when the players are busy with other games or activities and some persistent person springs his question without warning.

Santa's Bag

A tricky game for boys and girls with nimble wits! It can only be played, however, when the majority of the players are not familiar with it. Let the players sit in a circle. Start the game by saying, "Santa Claus packed his bag and in it he put —— ——." Mention some article that begins with the initials of your own name. I might say, "marshmallow bunnies," for example. Everyone must add something to the bag. If the object a player mentions does not start with his initials, he must sit on the floor. He gets his turn each time, but he may not again take his seat in the circle until he guesses the trick and discovers that Santa will not accept anything that does not start with his own initials.

Don't tell anybody the secret of the game. Avoid mentioning objects that are too far-fetched, or the others will learn the answer very quickly. Imagine the difficulty some of your friends with unusual names are going to have in thinking of different articles after the third or fourth round!

Blow Out the Christmas Candles

Arrange six red candles on a board or table. Number them as shown in the diagram. Players stand about 3 ft. away and take turns at "huffing and puffing" at the candles in an attempt to blow out the flames. Score as numbered and award an extra ten points for a "strike," that is, for blowing out all the candles in one blow.

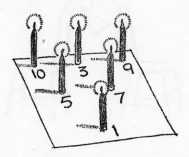

High scores are rare in this game. Players are usually laughing too hard to get up a "big wind" after seeing the facial contortions of their friends.

Clap In, Clap Out

Especially appropriate for Yuletide festivities is this veteran party game. Let one of the players leave the room. When he is gone, decide with the other players what he should do on his return. Think of something "Christmasy," like hanging a ball on the tree, putting a sprig of mistletoe in his lapel, or chugging like a toy train.

After you have decided on the action, signal the player to come back to the room. Without asking questions, he must perform as the group decided. The only help you and the others can give is to clap loudly when he is "hot" and to stamp when he is "cold." For example, as he approaches the Christmas tree, the clapping becomes very loud. When he turns away from it, the stamping starts. He turns back and sits under the tree. The clapping is faint then. He touches a ball, and it increases in tempo. Some hurrahs are added when he picks up the ball and starts tying it to the tree.

Ring the Bell for Christmas

In this game the players stand behind a throwing line and toss a bean bag at a bell suspended from a hoop tied between two chairs or hanging from the ceiling. To give it a Christmas air, cover the hoop with green paper and tie a red bow on the bell. Every time the bell rings the tosser scores a point.

Lawyer, Lawyer!

Let the players sit in two rows, facing each other. The individuals directly opposite are partners.

Choose a lawyer. One who can fire rapid questions will give the game a good start. The lawyer walks up and down between the lines. Without warning, he points to one of the players and shoots a question at him. BUT the answer must be given by that player's partner who is sitting directly opposite to him.

If this player fails to respond before the lawyer counts up to three, both he and his partner move to the last seats, while the other players move up. The object of the game is to reach the chairs at the head of the two rows and stay there. If a pair of partners can retain these first seats for five minutes they draw lots for the privilege of replacing the lawyer.

This can be a fast-moving action game if the lawyer keeps trapping victims with unexpected questions.

A Buffet Supper Table

This kind of party suggests an informal buffet supper, which is easy to arrange beforehand, and allows for an "elastic" meal-time.

For greater space, push the dining-table against the wall. You can then arrange at the back a fairly high table decoration which is effective, and which is at the same time well out of the way of the tempting supper dishes you wish to display.

Tall flowers are always charming, but not so easily found at this time of year. A striking and very pleasing effect, however, can be simply and inexpensively achieved. Your garden, or that of a friend, will afford an old branch of a tree. Choose a fairly symmetrical one, of tree-like shape. Prune it to the required size, clean it well, and distemper or paint it white. When the paint is almost dry, sprinkle some Christmas frost over it. Then, when the tree is quite dry, embed it firmly in a suitable-sized pot.

Arrange your frosty tree against the wall, concealing the pot in a bed of evergreens. You now have a perfect setting for the party favours, as well as an unusual decoration.

Fix red and green crackers all over it, and with gay ribbons hang small gifts from its branches. These may be inexpensive trifles or home-made sweets, and they look very festive if they are wrapped in brightly coloured cellophane bags.

At this time of year, and particularly if you have all been carolling or delivering your gifts, one or two hot dishes would be much appreciated. Arrange your table by placing a tureen of hot soup at one end, and serve tea, coffee, and hot spiced lemonade and hot mince pies at the other. Between these, arrange your assorted sandwiches and the tempting fruit salads, jellies, and trifles that make a buffet table so inviting.

See that the appropriate plates, forks, and spoons are placed beside the dishes of food, and ask one or two of your friends to assist in removing all used plates as quickly as possible.

Menu

Tomato soup	*Hot mince pies*
Scotch eggs with Russian salad	
Assorted sandwiches	
Apple snow	*Peach Melba*
Tea *Coffee*	*Hot spiced lemonade*

(For recipes for Peach Melba and Hot Spiced Lemonade see page 156.)

18
"Great Ambition" Party

THIS party idea came as a flash of inspiration to Susan the day she saw Joan push her cycle with one hand and, with the other, juggle a bottle filled with swimming tadpoles and river water.

"Been exploring again?"

"Uh-huh. Want to see my tadpoles?"

"No, they're ugly. When are you leaving for Africa?" asked Susan.

"In a couple of years. You wait and see."

Joan was the tomboy of the set and made no secret of her ambition to be an explorer. The girls liked her, even if they did think her a little "loony" when she disappeared on her "wild-life" jaunts into the woods and marshes.

But then every girl had her ambitions. So why not air them at a party? The thought flashed through Susan's mind as she watched Joan struggle on her way. She dashed over to Linda and Hazel, her closest pals. They thought it a great idea too, and immediately set to work planning this unique party. Here is the invitation they wrote on plain note-paper and dispatched to their friends:

Great Ambition Party

at

Susan's

July 30, 8 o'clock

> *Forget your inhibitions.*
> *Confess your great ambitions.*
> *Come as the girl you'd like to be*
> *When your future stars you've won.*
>
> *Put on the right attire;*
> *Be dancer, nurse, or flier.*
> *We'll have a ripping party*
> *That will whiz and zip with fun.*

Joan showed up in shorts with a pith helmet on her head, a knapsack on her back, and a butterfly net in her hand. Screams of laughter greeted her, and fresh peals rang out with each new arrival. Linda appeared in a ballet costume, and Jane in a nurse's uniform. Pauline, who wanted to be a doctor, wore a tailored suit and carried a leather case. There were teachers, aviators, a girl in hunting kit, and an automobile racer at the party.

The girls spent the first half-hour good-naturedly chaffing each other about their costumes and pet ambitions. Joan, a clown at heart, took the floor and gave a highly entertaining speech about the perils she had encountered on her last hunt for Big Game. Linda was persuaded to dance. And then, because everybody was in costume, it was decided that the perfect game to play would be *Actor Antics*. This is described in Chapter 15. Because their group was small, they formed three casts instead of four.

Prophecies followed next.

Prophecies

Susan distributed paper and pencils and told the girls to write the items she mentioned, in the following order:

1. A date—any time after 1950.
2. The name of one of the girls at the party. (Drawn from slips in a hat.)
3. A woman's profession.
4. A number.
5. A colour.
6. Another colour.
7. A sum of money.
8. An activity or pastime.
9. An article of clothing.
10. A flower.
11. Something to eat.
12. The name of a man.
13. An adjective.
14. A man's profession.
15. A number.
16. Another number.
17. An adverb.
18. Another adverb.
19. The name of a town or city.
20. An adjective.
21. A number.
22. A sum of money.

Lists were exchanged, and each girl had to read out her own prophecy, filling in the spaces with the corresponding items on the list. This was Hazel's:

In 1963, *Hazel West* will be a *film star*. She will weigh 20 pounds, have *pink* eyes and *green* hair, and will earn £20 a year. Her chief diversion will be *swatting flies*; her pet costume, a *bathing suit*; her favourite flower, a *petunia*; and her usual meal, a dish of *porridge*. In her work she will meet *John Wentworth*, a *beautiful opera star*, who stands 15 ft. tall, and tops the scale at 900 pounds. He will court her *coyly*, and propose *coldly*. They will elope to *Honolulu*, settle down to a *mad* life, and have 300 children. They will leave to their heirs the magnificent estate of *twopence*.

Who Am I?

Having just learned their futures, the girls now had to guess their immediate identities. To the back of each girl's dress Susan pinned the picture of a famous person. Some were living, some were dead, others taken from fiction. Among the personages represented were Madame Curie, Queen of Sheba, Ellen Terry, Lady Astor, Jane Austen, and Minnie Mouse. (If pictures are not available, write the names on slips of paper.)

Each girl tried to guess the name of the person whose picture was pinned to her back. They could ask questions which could be answered by "Yes" or "No." "Am I alive?" "Am I on the stage?" "Do I sing?" "Do I dance?" "Am I in the comic papers?" The questions grew rather wild before the game was over.

As soon as one of the girls guessed correctly, she was allowed to pin the picture to the front of her dress, and Susan pinned a different one on the back. The object was to collect the greatest number of pictures. Hazel was feeling especially bright that night. Within ten minutes she had eight pictures ornamenting her dress. No one else had nearly so many, so they accepted her as the undisputed champion famous lady of all time.

My Grandmother Likes

Grandmother is very fussy. She likes bread but not butter, tea but not coffee, honey but not jelly, oranges but not cherries.

This is one of those tricky guessing games that you spring on your friends with seeming innocence. Susan started it by saying, "My Grandmother likes chicks but not bunnies." Then the other girls took turns in mentioning something that grandmother would approve. Most of them did not know the game, and when they added something that grandmother disliked, they had to sit on the floor. Everyone continued listing grandmother's likes and dislikes, even the girls on the floor. When one of them caught on to the trick, she could again take her chair in the circle.

Have you guessed grandmother's idiosyncrasies? It's very easy. She likes everything but words with double consonants or vowels. That's why she likes tea but not does like *coffee*, and likes chicks but not *bunnies*. When you play the game, let every player repeat the sentence, "My grandmother likes —— but does not like ——."

Illustrated Biographies

This unusual game was the high point of Susan's Peep-into-the-Future Party. It is quite different from the ordinary hackneyed party games.

Each girl made an illustrated biography of one of the others. The facts were completely ridiculous, but the girls autographed each other's books and kept them as mementoes. Such souvenirs of good times with your friends are fun to have and to look at in later years. Perhaps the books may even be prophetic. There's no telling. Joan might become a famous woman explorer and Linda a great dancer. Think what fun it would be then for Susan to have in her possession a souvenir of the party at which these two confessed their pet ambitions.

For the game you will need a pile of old magazines, some sheets of heavy wrapping paper, a ball of twine, and several tubes of paste, boxes of crayons, and pairs of scissors. Write the names of all the guests on slips of paper, shuffle them, then let each girl draw one slip from the pile. That is the name of the girl whose biography she is to write. The name is kept secret until the book is completed. If a girl should draw her own name, the slip must be returned to the pile after she has chosen another.

Each girl makes an illustrated book. Cut the pages from brown wrapping paper and fasten them together with twine. The books should contain eight pages, not including the covers. Each one is devoted to one of the following events in a girl's life:

1. Birthplace.	5. Her chief activity.
2. Baby days.	6. Her first sweetheart.
3. First day in school.	7. Her ambition.
4. Schoolgirl crushes.	8. Her future.

Biographers search through the magazines for pictures illustrating these milestones in their subject's life. Below each picture they write descriptive captions. These should be as short as possible, not more than twenty-five words. The book Joan compiled for Linda contained this:

1. In this stately mansion the wee Linda was born. (Picture of a tumbled-down shack.)

2. She was a pretty, but a fussy baby. (Picture of a howling baby.)

3. She was always studious and could hardly wait for her first day in school. (Picture of a tearful little girl holding her mother's dress.)

4. A glamour girl at ten, these were her admirers. (A row of comic-strip characters.)

5. This was always her favourite sport. (Picture of a girl lying on a sofa with a magazine in one hand and a bar of chocolate in the other.)

6. Her first sweetheart was her only real love. (A picture of Micky Mouse.)

7. But she turned him down to become a dancer. (Picture of a tired ballet dancer.)

8. Her success was great, but she did not like the life of the theatre, and finally decided to stand for Parliament. (Picture of a woman making a soap-box oration.)

Enlarge the books if you wish, and include pictures of amusing incidents which might have happened to your friends. After the books have been completed, each girl reads her own biography aloud. Each one surpasses its predecessor in absurdity.

By the time the giggles subside, your friends will be ready for refreshments. At least, Susan's were.

THE PARTY TABLE

How on earth would you decorate a table for a "Great Ambition" Party? Susan hadn't the slightest notion. She wanted something really different, and was beginning to feel discouraged, when her mother came to the rescue.

"What do people in stories do with their ambitions and dreams, Susan? Don't you remember about 'Hitching your wagon to a star'?"

"Wagons and stars!" That was it. "We could have little wagons at each place," Susan said excitedly, "and a big star in the middle of the table."

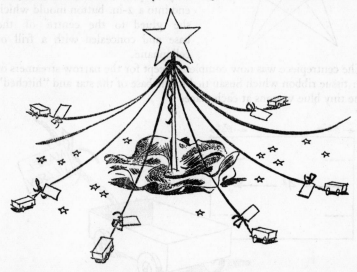

That was all the help Susan needed. From there on the table was her own creation. And it was a great success. The girls thought it the prettiest they had ever seen.

The table was covered with pale blue crêpe paper. Over this Susan threw a filmy cloth of white muslin, sprinkled with gummed silver stars.

On each side of the centrepiece stood two slim white candles in flat holders that were covered with cellophane frills. The base of the centrepiece was oval, made of plain cardboard, 12 in. by 16 in. Susan covered this with blue crêpe paper and then pasted to the top side three full ruffles of cellophane of the same colour.

Rising from this glittering base was a large silver star, measuring 8½ in. from point to point. Susan had a little difficulty with the star. She could not find a large enough one in the shops, and she could not manage to draw a perfect shape. Then she tried placing a smaller star on cardboard, and enlarging it by making dots the same distance away from each of the five points, and from the bases of the triangles that formed the star. This scheme worked. So Susan

drew her larger star, cut it from cardboard, and glued it to a wire stem 15 in. long. To make the stem strong enough she twisted together four strands of wire. This she covered with a diagonal strip of blue crêpe paper, and then inserted one end into a 2-in. button mould which she glued to the centre of the base and concealed with a frill of cellophane.

The centrepiece was now complete except for the narrow streamers of silver tissue ribbon which Susan tied to the base of the star and "hitched" to the tiny blue wagons at each place.

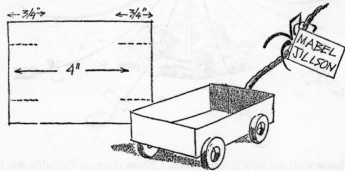

Each wagon was made from a piece of kindergarten paper, $3\frac{1}{2}$ in. by 4 in. Susan cut two $\frac{3}{4}$-in. slits into both ends, then folded back the sides and end pieces and pasted them into place. Four peppermint wheels and a pipe-cleaner handle were glued to each wagon. To hide the fuzzy surface of the pipe cleaners, Susan covered the handles with tinfoil. Place cards were tied to the tips, and the wagons filled with white sweets.

Menu

Minced ham, Egg and cress sandwiches
Apple and Orange salad   Small fruit tarts
Lemonade or Fruit punch
(Recipe for Apple and Orange Salad on page 156.)

A BOY'S BIRTHDAY PARTY
19

MOST boys prefer manly sports, and vigorous, strenuous games. Their idea of fun is to kick a ball or test their batting skill. They like parties, too, but most parties are such pink-tea, sissy stuff, that the boys would rather stay at home.

Well, here's one designed just for them. It does not include football or cricket, since it is an indoor party. The games, however, are the tough-fibred kind on which boys like to sharpen their wits, and there are some rough-and-ready stunts which appeal to the masculine sense of humour.

Plan the table decorations round the hobbies of the host or individual guests—sports, boats, trains, or planes. Most boys are air-minded these days, so an aeronautical setting is usually a safe choice. A hangar makes an attractive centrepiece. A realistic one can be made very easily from white kindergarten paper. Tie a ribbon from the top to the electric light fitment, but do not fasten the top of the hangar to the sides. At

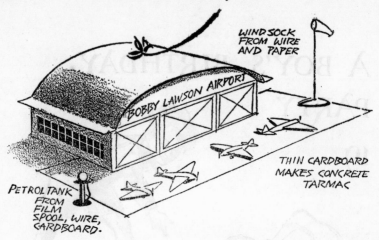

dessert time, the roof can be lifted by pulling the ribbon, revealing inside the birthday cake or a pile of favours.

If the hangar centrepiece is used, small planes can be scattered over the table. Model plane assembly kits would make appropriate favours.

Air Control

An inch is not as good as a mile when you are flying. The ability to judge distances accurately sometimes makes the difference between life and death in the air. This knowledge prompted one of my young friends, who would rather talk about aircraft than eat, to devise this game.

A squadron leader places a plane some distance from a line. The other players then guess the distance of the plane from the line. To win, the player must guess correctly within a fraction of an inch. The leader moves the plane and the boys guess once more. Peter and his friends play the game for hours. Try your own skill at it.

Air Objective

In this game, grounded pilots bet which plane in the air will be the first to reach its objective. Six toy aircraft make up the squadron. Each one flies a straight course from the home field to its goal. Number the planes, and chalk six lanes on the floor. (If you can't mark the floor, use a long strip of linoleum or wrapping paper.) Draw lines across the lanes so that there are twenty squares for each plane. These are the hops the planes make before refuelling.

Place an obstacle in each lane to represent fog banks which delay the planes even longer. Appoint a mechanic to move the planes, place three dice in a cup, and you are ready to start.

The squadron leader rolls the dice and the planes bearing the numbers thrown move forward one space. If he throws a 3, 2, and 6, these planes advance one square. If a 4 and two 5's come up, No. 4 plane advances one square, and No. 5 moves forward two spaces. When a plane hits a fog bank, a double must be thrown before the plane can go forward.

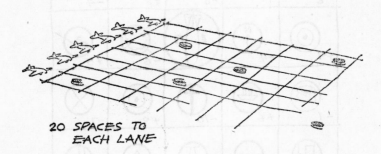

20 SPACES TO
EACH LANE

Bets of beans or play money may be placed with the squadron leader before the planes take off. In exchange, the bettor should receive a ticket bearing the number of the plane on which he places his bet. The player who collects most beans after several flights wins the game.

Bombardment

Here's an exciting game for air enthusiasts. Draw the accompanying chart on plywood or stiff cardboard, using a different colour for each symbol.

Players take turns at throwing darts at the targets. Each is allowed to throw five darts at a time. Score the points indicated. Darts should be used only if it is possible to support the target against a blank wall and to fence off the area between the target and the person throwing. Unless these precautions are taken, painful and sometimes serious accidents may occur. If there is any question about their safety at your particular party, eliminate the darts entirely and let the players pin small paper planes to the target while they are blindfolded.

Key to chart.

+ 1 Stand by.	— 1 Fog bound.
+ 2 Scramble.	— 2 Engine failure.
+ 3 Dispersal point.	— 3 Pancake.
+ 4 Advance base.	— 4 Navigation error.
+ 5 Report troop action.	— 5 Out of petrol.
+ 6 Report fleet action.	— 6 Ack-ack.
+ 7 Objective photographed.	— 7 Target missed.
+ 8 Enemy disabled.	— 8 Hospital.
+ 9 Enemy shot down.	— 9 Captured.
+10 Objective destroyed.	—10 Down in flames.

Airborne

This is an old-time stunt which can only be used on unsuspecting victims. It should be a great success with uninitiated, would-be fliers.

Take the victims to another room. Then place both ends of an ironing board, or a board of similar size, on several books or blocks of wood. This will raise the board several inches from the ground.

The pilot stands on the centre of the board. An assistant is at each end. The blindfolded victims are brought in one at a time and told that they are going for a flight. The pilot helps the passenger to step up on the board and tells him to place his hands on the pilot's shoulders.

The assistants make the sound of whirring engines and lift the board an inch or so, jiggling it slightly while they are raising it. Meanwhile the pilot stoops down slowly. When he gets so low that the passenger has trouble in keeping his hands on the pilot's shoulders, the latter shouts, "Bail out." Even the most daring will be seized with momentary panic when they are told to jump, for the sensation of being in mid-air is most realistic. It takes a good deal of courage to jump 6 ft. when you are blindfolded. But the brave will hold their breath and take a mighty leap, only to discover that they were no more than 6 in. off the ground.

To add to the illusion of flying while the stunt is in progress, the pilot should call out, "Watch out for that light"; "Don't bump your head on the ceiling"; "Mind the light."

Ping-Pong Hockey

This is an excellent party game, played the same as *Feather Football* (see Games List), except that the players fan a ping-pong ball with a card instead of blowing a feather.

Apple Bowls

Set up nine apples on tripod bases, made by sticking three cocktail sticks into the bottom of the apples. Arrange them in the regular diamond form as you would ninepins. Score as in ninepins, rolling three apples or rubber balls per turn, or make up your own scoring system.

I Went to France

You'll need a good long memory to remain in this game. One person starts by saying, "I went to France and I took with me an antelope." The second person repeats the sentence, mentions what the first person took and adds another object that starts with "A." Each player in turn repeats what has gone before and adds something to the list of items taken on the trip. Every object must start with the letter "A" until someone misses. That player is then eliminated from the game, and the following person starts a new list, this time choosing words that begin with "B."

Continue through the alphabet if you can. End the game when only three players are left.

Indoor Golf

If you can restrain your enthusiasm for hitting long drives, you can have an amusing game of indoor golf without breaking lamps or vases. Use a golf club or a cane and a tennis ball. Lay out the course over adjoining rooms. Golfers must shoot round, not over, such hazards as couches, desks, and chairs. Here are four holes you might have on your course.

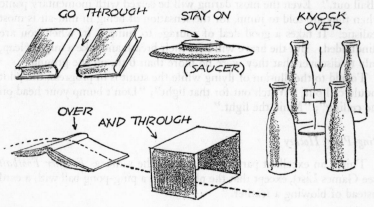

GO THROUGH   STAY ON   KNOCK OVER

(SAUCER)

OVER   AND THROUGH

Ghosts

This game probably gets its name from the fact that eliminated players haunt the individuals who are still playing, trying to trap them into speaking to the ghosts and becoming "spooks" themselves.

The object of the game is to add letters to words without finishing them. Suppose Joe starts the game and says "C." John, who is sitting next to him, adds the letter "A." Bill adds "T." That spells *cat*. Three-letter words are permitted, but after the third letter has been added, any player who completes a word becomes a third of a Ghost. If the next letters happen to be "T" and "L," the sixth player must add the "E" unless he can think of some other word besides *cattle* which can be formed with the previous letters. As a penalty, he becomes a third of a Ghost.

A player must always have some word in mind when he mentions a letter. He does not have to tell what it is, however, unless the succeeding player challenges him. Then if there is no such word, or if he was bluffing, he becomes a third of a Ghost. The player who issued the challenge starts a new word.

As soon as a player is a whole Ghost, he is no longer permitted to form words, but he is not entirely eliminated from the game. He sits around and heckles the other players. If he can trap anyone into speaking to him, that person becomes a third of a Ghost, or a whole Ghost if he is already two-thirds of one. The "haunting" and the heckling make this one of the liveliest and most popular games in the party repertoire.

Deer Hunt

Although only two boys at a time play this game, it is packed with fun and suspense for the spectators and participants.

One boy is appointed the Hunter; the other, the Deer. They stand at opposite ends of a table. Both are blindfolded. When the starting signal is given, the hunter stalks the deer round the table and attempts to catch him. The latter tries to avoid capture. The room must be very quiet so that the two can hear each other's movements. But sometimes it is difficult to restrain a shout of laughter when you see the hunter and deer cautiously creeping towards each other and then turn and go in opposite directions when they are almost in each other's arms.

If the hunter wishes, he may occasionally rap on the table to frighten the deer. Of course, this gives the deer the hunter's position. Sometimes the hunter's rap is ill-timed. The deer may be creeping up to meet him just when he hears the knock. In a split second, he is travelling fast in the opposite direction, and the hunter has to start again. When the hunter catches the deer, two other boys take their places.

The King has Toothache

Choose one boy to be King. He sits at one end of the room. Next to him are several empty chairs. The king is blindfolded. Furthermore, he has toothache and does not want to be disturbed. The other players are stationed at the opposite end of the room. One at a time they try to steal across the room and sit in one of the chairs next to the king. If the king hears any movement he groans, and the boy who was tiptoeing across the room must sit on the floor. He may not again try to reach the king until all the other players have been caught or one of them has managed to sit in the chair next to the king without being detected. This boy then takes the king's place, and the game is repeated.

20

TREASURE HUNT PARTY

H ERE'S an impromptu, out-of-doors party.
Get on the telephone and summon your friends, or scrawl notes on brown wrapping paper. Tell them all to wear their sturdiest walking shoes and to meet you at your house at a certain time. Don't give any more information. A little mystery adds to the fun.

They will gather—probably ahead of time—wondering what kind of cross-country hike or paper-chase you have "up your sleeve." When you are all assembled, toss numbered slips into a hat and let the guests draw for partners. Then give each couple a bag to carry the booty, a pencil, and a slip of paper containing these instructions:

"You and your partner are off on a hunt for treasure. Find as many of the following articles as you can collect, beg, or borrow. Go anywhere you like, but be back in an hour. The treasure will be counted, and the prizes awarded. Anyone not on hand will be eliminated from the game.

1. Two drinking straws.
2. Three different kinds of match-box covers.
3. Two 'blonde' hair pins.
4. Three knitting needles.
5. An onion.
6. A safety-razor blade.
7. A bus ticket with the number 7 on it.
8. A 2-in. nail.
9. Three white round stones.
10. A white rubber eraser.
11. Four milk-bottle caps.
12. Two cinema-ticket stubs.
13. Five different sizes of safety-pins.
14. The number of steps at Mr. John Brown's front entrance.
15. The number of trees on the pavement outside No. 10 Water St.
16. The date on the cornerstone of St. John's Church.
17. The comic strip from last Sunday's paper.
18. The exact wording of the sign on Jones' Hardware Store."

(Substitute local names and addresses where necessary.)

The searchers start off at full speed. Their first call will probably be at their own homes, but for most of the objects and information they will have to do some real foot-work and live-wire "detecting."

When the couples return, they deposit their booty and a judge checks it over. Get ready for some wild stories. Hunters outstrip even fishermen in their tales of the "one almost caught." Let the story-tellers have free rein. This "spinning of yarns" that grow twice as big in the telling is the best part of the Treasure Hunt.

Award inexpensive prizes to the winning couples. Then serve the eats. Appetites will be ravenous, so have plenty of food that is easy to prepare and serve. What does that suggest? Hot sausage rolls and potato crisps? Of course! Could anything be more tempting?

In keeping with the uniqueness of the party, serve the meal in lunch-counter style. Detail two boys to heat the sausage rolls and crisps. Fit them out with white aprons and crêpe-paper hats. Let the girls act as waitresses, decked out in perky crêpe-paper caps and frilly aprons.

Arrange the food on tables in the kitchen, pushed together in counter style. Use a white wrapping-paper cover. Set the counter with stacks of paper plates, dishes of sweets, potato crisps, relishes, split rolls, and bread and butter. The simplest and tastiest sweet for this lunch-counter meal is ice cream in paper cups. Serve tea, cocoa, and fruit drinks.

21

A VALENTINE PARTY *modern style*

ARE you a St. Valentine's child? What an opportunity for giving a 14th of February birthday party that will be "different," and yet full of fun and frolic in the most up-to-date style! The present-day St. Valentine puts a smile and a chuckle into his romances, so, while taking advantage of the day to air one or two of the old customs, stress the humorous rather than the romantic side.

In the true valentine manner, your invitations should be gaily coloured —and anonymous, as far as practicable. Be sure, however, to give your address very clearly. In cases where this is not sufficient indication of your identity, you will have to sign the invitation.

VALENTINE GAMES

Odd or Even?

Start off the evening with this romping guessing and trading game. It is a good party-opener, and will keep the first-comers entertained while you are waiting for the rest of the guests. Provide each player with ten sugar hearts. No, not for eating! At least not until the end of the game. The hearts are used as counters and are concealed in the players' hands while they try to get the others to guess whether they are holding in the right hand an odd or an even number.

Suppose, for example, that Frances, who is holding four hearts in her right hand, and the extra ones in her left, decides to corner David. She goes up to him, extends her right hand, and asks, "Odd or even?" Unluckily for David, he says, "Odd." Frances opens her hand, shows him her hearts, and collects two from David. That is the required penalty for each wrong guess, with the one exception noted later. To make up his loss, David goes after Peter to see if he can capture some of Peter's hearts. If David had happened to guess correctly, Frances would have had to forfeit to him all the hearts she was holding in her right hand.

A penalty is always collected, except when a player is reduced to his last heart. This he is allowed to keep, so that he may remain in the game and continue challenging others.

Sir Valentine has Lost his Hat

Number the chairs for this game. There should be one less than the number of players. The person who is left without a chair starts the game by addressing the person in the fourth chair as follows:

LEADER: "Sir Valentine has lost his hat. Have you seen it, Number Four, Sir?"
NUMBER FOUR: "Who, Sir? I, Sir?"
LEADER: "Yes, Sir, you, Sir."
NUMBER FOUR: "No, Sir! Not I, Sir."
LEADER: "Who then, Sir?"
NUMBER FOUR: "Number Eight, Sir."

As soon as the player sitting in the eighth chair hears his number mentioned, he must ask:

NUMBER EIGHT: "Who, Sir? I, Sir?"
LEADER: "Yes, Sir. You, Sir."
NUMBER EIGHT: "No, Sir. Not I, Sir."
LEADER: "Who then, Sir?"
NUMBER EIGHT: "Number so-and-so, Sir."

The dialogue continues with a different player each time until someone fails to give an immediate answer, makes a mistake in wording, or answers out of turn. Anyone making such a mistake must move to the last chair in the line, all those formerly below him moving up one chair. The object of the game is to reach the first chair and remain there.

If you wish, you can change the leader each time a mistake is made, making the player in error become leader, the former leader taking the last chair in the row.

Remember that the chairs are numbered, not the players. That's where the fun and confusion come in. When a player has concentrated very hard on being Number Three, and then suddenly has to move up to chair Number Two, it is easy to catch him off guard.

Name the Other

How many couples, renowned in legend and story, can you pair off with their mates? Here's a game to test your friends' knowledge of famous "twosomes." Read the first of each pair of names, one by one, and let the players call out the proper mates. No one minds if you mention a few of whom they have never heard—and you might include a few couples known only to your own crowd.

Award a sugar heart to the first person to give the correct answer, and an inexpensive prize to the player who collects the most hearts.

Romeo—Juliet.
David Copperfield—Dora.
Pierrot—Pierrette.
Samson—Delilah.
Napoleon—Josephine.
Venus—Adonis.
Antony—Cleopatra.
King George—Queen Elizabeth.
Peter Pan—Wendy.
Lancelot—Elaine.

King Arthur—Guinevere.
Captain John Smith—Pocahontas.
Popeye—Olive Oyle.
Hero—Leander.
Mickey Mouse—Minnie.
Jack—Jill.
Dante—Beatrice.
Hansel—Gretel.
Punch—Judy.
Tristan—Isolde.

Find the Leader

How good are you at quick imitations? Can you watch another person out of the corner of your eye and follow his actions so quickly that no one can catch you looking at him? Try this game and see.

Players sit in a circle. One is chosen to be "It." He leaves the room and a second person is selected to perform various actions in rapid-fire succession—stamp his feet, wriggle his fingers, pat his head, anything he can think of.

The others try to imitate the leader's actions, but try not to reveal to "It" who is starting them. "It" returns to the room, and by watching the various players, tries to discover the leader's identity. The player who inadvertently makes it known takes "It's" place.

When the latter leaves the room, appoint a new leader and repeat the game.

Catch and Answer

This is another high-speed guessing game. Begin the fun by tossing a ball to one of the players. At the same time call out a question which he must immediately answer. Who was last year's boat-race winner? Who won the last Ashes? Who are the Anzacs? Who is the present woman tennis champion?

Ask any question you can think of and then start counting. Before you reach ten, the person to whom you have thrown the ball must catch or recover it, then answer your question. If he is quick enough to do so, he scores a point. Whether he adds to his score or not, he has the next turn at throwing the ball and firing a question at some other player. Keep the ball rolling and the questions flying at high speed and you will have a game that hums with action.

Honeymoon Relay

The ridiculous appearance of the players in the funny attire they are required to wear during the relay makes this one of the most hilarious of party games.

You cannot have a honeymoon without a bride and groom, so let the players draw numbered slips from a hat to find their mates. Then form teams for a partner relay, and provide each group with a shopping bag or a suitcase containing a necktie, a voluminous dress, an apron, a floppy hat, a bandana, a vest, or whatever articles of clothing you would like to toss into the collection. The contents of the suitcases may vary, but each should contain the same number of articles.

At the starting signal, the first couple in each team opens the suitcase, dons the apparel, then closes the bag and runs in the outlandish costumes to a goal at the far end of the room. There they take off their borrowed finery, replace it in the suitcase, run back to the starting place, and hand the closed valise to the next couple.

All the couples in each team repeat the same performance. When the last one in any group returns to the starting line, the game is won for that side.

Secrets

When could you have a better excuse than on St. Valentine's Day to pry good-naturedly into the romantic secrets of your friends? Foolish, nonsensical secrets, to be sure, but no end of fun when they are unwittingly revealed. Provide paper and pencils and ask the players to write the items you request in the following order:

1. Name of one of the players. (*Girls write boys' names, boys write girls'.*)
2. A statement. (He or she said ——.)
3. Another statement. (You said ——.)
4. A place.
5. An article or dish of food.
6. A sum of money.
7. A time of day.
8. A statement.
9. Answer "Yes" or "No."
10. A wish or desire.
11. Answer "Yes" or "No."
12. Name of a player. (*Boys write girls' names, girls write boys'.*)
13. Answer "Yes" or "No."
14. An exclamation of enthusiasm or distaste.

Each player in turn reads the answers he has written as you ask these questions:

1. Whom did you meet last night?
2. What did he (or she) say?
3. What did you say?
4. Where did you go?
5. What did you have to eat?
6. How much money did you spend?
7. At what time did you arrive home?
8. What did your mother say?
9. Did you care?
10. What is your ambition?
11. Will you attain it?
12. Whom do you love?
13. Does he (or she) love you?
14. What do you think of this game?

Blarney Stammer

You have probably heard the legend of the Blarney Stone. The large hewn rock is in Blarney Castle. Tradition says that anyone who kisses it receives the gift of golden speech—the "gift of the gab," some cynics say.

Let the players sit in a circle and choose one of them to be "It." When a player least expects to be called on, "It" points to him and shouts a letter of the alphabet. Within one minute, that player must quickly recite all the words he can think of which begin with the given letter. If "It" says, "B," the player to whom he pointed might rattle off in quick succession, "Bats, belfry, battle, butter, bacon, bomber, bing, bang, bat, bung."

Time the players and count the words. Anyone who fails to give ten words before "It" says, "Stammer, stammer, Blarney Stone," forfeits some personal possession and cannot reclaim it until he has paid a specified penalty. Place the loot thus acquired in a hat.

Now choose one person to be the judge and jury, and let him sit on a chair in the centre of the room. Stand behind him and hold the forfeited articles over his head, one at a time. Repeat the following dialogue for each one:

"Heavy, heavy hangs over thy head," you say to the Judge. "What shall the owner do to redeem it?"

The judge asks, "Fine or Superfine?"

Answer "Fine" if the article belongs to a boy, "Superfine" if it is a girl's. The judge mentions the stunt that must be performed, or the penalty that the owner must pay to get it back. Here's his opportunity for good-natured jokes and jovial tricks. A quick-witted judge can make the game lots of fun.

One of the favourite party pranks years ago was to command some shy young man to "Say whom you love the best." After much stuttering and stammering he would confess his love, only to have the judge say that would not do. Again the judge would command him, "Say whom you love the best." Once more the poor victim would try. Finally it would occur to him that all the judge was asking him to do was to repeat the words "whom you love the best." But by that time the whole party knew the object of the victim's secret affection.

Here are some other amusing *Forfeits*:

Push a penny the length of the room with one's nose.

Walk in a straight line looking through the wrong end of a telescope or pair of field glasses.

Eat a biscuit, then whistle a tune.

Imitate one or more farmyard cries.

Kneel on the floor and repeat the Siamese college yell, "O—Wa—Ta—Goo—Siam!"

TABLE DECORATIONS FOR A PARTY OF GIRLS OR FOR A MIXED GROUP

These coquettish pierrette dolls, in their gay red-and-white dresses and heart-decorated hats, make charming table figures for a party of girls, or of boys and girls together.

The centre figure is dainty, feminine, and so very graceful that you never would guess that her body is only a milk bottle, and her head a lemon. A regular doll could be dressed in the same way. But if you do not have a doll of the right size, and do not want to go to the trouble of making a wire frame for one, just set to work with your milk bottle, lemon, and crêpe paper, and your centrepiece pierratte will be completed in a few seconds.

Thrust a short lollipop stick into the lemon. This will keep the head in place. Before fastening the lemon to the milk bottle, however, give your doll a delicate pink-tinted complexion by covering the lemon with an under-layer of peach crêpe paper and over that a square of transparent cellophane. Paste the crêpe paper to the lemon at the back of the head, but gather the cellophane and tie it at the top where the cap will hide the ends.

Paint the eyes and mouth with poster paint or cut them from gummed seals. Add a red frill to conceal the folds of the cellophane at the base of the lemon. The simplest way to do this is to run a tacking thread through one edge of a strip of red crêpe paper, 20 in. long and 2 in. wide. Draw the thread so that the paper will form a ruffle, and tie it in place.

The head is now ready to be inserted into the milk bottle. Push the lollipop stick through a hole punched in the milk-bottle cap. Fasten a button mould to the end of the stick to keep the head firm, and then place the cap inside the neck of the bottle.

The dress is a bouffant mass of red-and-white fringe. Fold together a strip of red and a strip of white crêpe paper, each measuring 10 in. by 60 in. Fringe both ends of the double strip, one to a depth of 8 in., the other to a depth of 1 in. Gather the uncut part round the neck in such a way that the shorter ends will frame the face. If the skirt requires extra fullness, add an over-skirt 9 in. in width. Fringe the bottom end to a depth of 8 in., but leave the top edge uncut. Gather the latter and tie it over the underskirt. The frilled collar will hide the join.

The doll can be given extra height by standing it on a book or an inverted soup plate covered with red crêpe paper. If you do this, lengthen the skirt accordingly.

The doll's arms are two pipe cleaners, tied in place just under the collar. Paste two joined hearts to the end of one; and to the other, narrow white streamers dangling with hearts. For a more lavish— though not extravagant—effect let the doll hold in this hand the ends of heart-decorated streamers which trail across the table and hang over the edge.

The clown-type hat is made from a straight band of white crêpe paper, 4½ in. by 5½ in. Fringe one edge and fold the other back to form a ¼-in. band. Before tying the top together, insert a narrow strip of red fringe to give the pom-pom effect. Decorate the front with three red hearts.

To outward appearances, the individual pierrettes holding place cards and acting as favours are smaller duplicates of the centrepiece doll. The heads, however, are 1-in. pale pink sweets covered with cellophane; the body is a 5-in. lollipop stick; and the bases are made of 2-in. button moulds.

Dresses and hats are exactly the same as those for the larger doll, with the following differences in measurements: Skirt, $5\frac{1}{2}$ in. by 12 in.; the narrow fringe, 1 in.; the deeper edge, 4 in.; hat, 2 in. by $2\frac{3}{4}$ in.

Supper Menu

Heart-shaped sandwiches

Funny-faced pies   *Bunny-rabbit salad*

Assorted biscuits   *Jellies and cream*

Fruit punch with decorated ice cubes

Dishes of old-fashioned "conversation" lozenges

(For Recipes, see page 157.)

22   CIRCUS PARTY

IF you are planning a party on a large scale, e.g. for school, club, or
for any occasion when you are faced with the problem of entertaining
a crowd of bright and active youngsters, give a Circus Party as an
amusing novelty.

It is always grand fun. It is colourful, exciting, and brimful of laughs
and surprises. It requires a certain amount of organizing, but there are
few better ways of catering for a large number of children, for various
activities can be carried on simultaneously. Also, with a few adaptations,
it can be made the ideal summer garden party.

Send invitations in the form of circus posters:

THE CIRCUS IS COMING TO TOWN

Clowns

◆

Jugglers

Animal Acts

THE
Most COLOSSAL, Most STUPENDOUS
Most BREATHTAKING
SPECTACLE IN THE WORLD!

Invitation : *Each person who enters our big circus ring*
Must juggle, do tricks, or dance, tumble, or sing.
So dress as a snake charmer, clown, or a goop,
And come and perform with the rest of the troupe.

Brightly coloured ribbon streamers; red, yellow, and blue balloons; and gaudy pennants will give the party room the lively spirit of the circus big-top.

The host should be the ringmaster. It is his job to introduce the acts, make elaborate announcements, and keep the show running at a speedy pace. He may wear riding breeches and snap his whip in a bossy manner, or he may be attired in evening clothes, with a red ribbon across his chest and medals dangling from his lapel.

A few grown-ups are a necessity. They should keep discreetly in the background, but should nevertheless be well primed in their duties as potential referees and advisers. Even the most carefully worked-out programme is seldom free from unexpected problems and hitches, and you may be glad of a little adult advice. The party described here is for an informal home or club gathering to which guests are invited to come in costume, prepared to perform a circus stunt. Fun is spontaneous, and performances increase in liveliness as the circus spirit warms up.

The performances which the guests contribute to the programme will probably keep the party humming, but if there should be a lull, here are some amusing stunts which you can put on with little preparation.

Tight-rope Walker

Stretch a white string across the floor. Hold a parasol in one hand and walk on the string as you would if it were 20 ft. off the ground, going through all the fancy motions of the professional tight-rope walker.

Upside-down Singers

Let two boys stretch a sheet between them, some distance away from the spectators. Three or four girls or boys stand behind it and put stockings on their arms and shoes on their hands. Explain to the audience that the curtain is necessary because these unusual individuals can sing only while they are standing on their heads. The performers then raise their arms and wave them in time to the song they sing. The effect is always startling and brings shouts of laughter, even though it may take the audience only a moment to guess what is going on behind the sheet.

Strong Man

The comic strong man wears a suit of long underwear or tights, padded with bulges of cloth or cotton-wool to give the appearance of

over-developed muscles. With great effort he lifts black boxes of different sizes, marked: 100 lb., 500 lb., and 1,000 lb. After he has picked
up the last one with superhuman effort, a caretaker arrives and sweeps
them away, much to the strong man's discomfort.

Midget Wonder

While the boys are still holding the curtain, place a table behind it.
Drape the front so that the legs and feet of the performers are completely
concealed.

Two individuals are needed for the stunt. One has stockings on his
arms and shoes on his hands. The other wears a loose cape or a dress
with a full skirt. He may also wear a bonnet or a hair ribbon. This
person stands behind the table.

The other stoops down behind him, and extends his arms so that his
elbows rest on the standing player's hips, and his arms and hands are on
the table. Arrange the cape in such a way that this performer is completely hidden from view and the midget seems to be sitting on the table.

When the curtain opens, the midget converses with the audience.
The person who has his stocking-covered arms on the table can provoke
a lot of laughs by crossing his arms when they should be straight, raising
one to scratch the midget's head with his shoes, and finally waving both
in the air.

Dead-shot Dick

This amazing cowboy can shoot a biscuit out of the mouth of his assistant while standing on his head, shooting from the hip or between his legs. The biscuit always falls as the pistol cracks. Have you guessed why? At just the right moment his assistant bites the biscuit.

The stunt never fails to amuse the audience if the cowboy convincingly carries off his act and pretends to shoot from difficult angles.

Operation Stunt

Stretch a sheet across the room. Behind it place a long table and behind that a floor lamp or table lamp which can be adjusted so that the light will throw the shadow of the table and the performers on the sheet.

The patient lies on the table. The doctor stands at the side of the table and bends over the sick man. Another person in front of the screen describes the operation while the doctor removes from the patient strings of spaghetti, a clanking chain, an alarm clock, and other ridiculous objects which the patient is supposed to have swallowed.

All these objects are lying on the table behind the patient, but the shadows thrown on the screen as the doctor picks them up convey the impression that he is removing them directly from the patient's stomach.

CLOWN CAPERS

Clowns are the life of any circus. They can also be the life of your party if the madcaps in your crowd let themselves go with some of the following antics:

A clown runs away from a broomstick tied to his coat tail.

Another clown dances with a dummy, the shoes of which are pinned to the clown's shoes, and one arm round his neck.

A third clown makes a great show of performing a dive from the top of a ladder into a bucket or small tub. After several dramatic, near take-offs, another clown rushes in and removes the bucket in the nick of time.

One-man Orchestra.—A clown hangs a washboard and some pots and pans round his middle. With a toy trumpet tied to a string round his neck, and with thimbles on his fingers, the clown plays "hot" music on his kitchen instruments.

Clown Battle.—Two clowns start a fierce fight. The struggle continues until one of them suddenly puts his hand to his mouth, runs to a corner and spits his teeth on the floor. His supposed teeth are white beans.

Boxing Bout.—Two blindfolded clowns put boxing gloves on their right hands. In their left they hold tin cans filled with pebbles. These are rattled to inform opponents of their positions. When the boxers think they are near enough, they exchange blows. Without the boxers' knowledge, the referee also has a tin can. He rattles it to distract the boxers and puts in an occasional blow of his own. Before the count of nine, the bout is a general free-for-all.

You can supplement this list *ad lib.* with tricks from your own repertoire.

SIDE-SHOWS AND OTHER WONDERS

In planning your circus, don't forget the side-show freaks and attractions—the snake charmer, the Hawaiian dancers, and—

The Siamese Twins	Two girls inside a woman's dress.
The Headless Wonder	A boy with an overcoat buttoned over his head.
The Glass-eater	A girl munching crystal rock.
The Ten-foot Giant	A boy on stilts.
The Fat Lady	A girl padded with pillows, wearing a voluminous dress.
The Walking Skeleton	A boy wearing a suit of underwear dyed black, with ribs and bones painted in white.
The Bearded Lady	A girl with whiskers pasted to her chin.

AMUSEMENT PARK

The amusement park is a popular spot in the circus grounds before and after the show. The exciting games described below can all be made with equipment which can be found around the house. They will be fun to play before your own circus stunt or while you are waiting for supper.

The first, second, and fourth games can be set up on chairs. Write directions on placards, and place them next to each game so that you will not have to repeat the rules continually. Provide each player with a score card. Let all the guests go through the complete circuit. The games can be played simultaneously, in any order. Award a prize to the boy or girl who scores the most points.

Make a Date

Place a large calendar on a chair or table. From a distance of 6 ft. players toss five milk-bottle tops on to the calendar. Their score is the total sum of the dates on which the tops land. If a top rests on a line, the larger number counts.

Egg-box Toss

Number the sections of an egg box. Players stand 5 ft. away and toss beans or pennies into the box. The numbers on the sections determine the score.

Tiddley Winks Goal

Construct a small goal of lollipop sticks or pipe cleaners. Place the goal in the centre of the table and mark a starting line at one end. From this line, players try to snap tiddley winks over the goal. Score six points for each goal.

Ringer

Place a carton on a table or chair, bottom-side up. Insert five clothes pegs. Allow a large section of the clothes peg to extend above the carton. From a line 8 ft. away players try to ring the clothes pegs with rubber rings. Score ten points for a ringer, and allow each player ten throws.

Roll 'em In

Stand a cardboard carton so that the bottom is facing the player. Cut four or five slits in the carton. Players try to roll pennies into the slits. Each has five trials. This game is best played on a table or smooth floor.

Potato Golf

Mark three concentric circles on the floor with chalk or string. Wire hoops can also be used. Use a cane for a stick and try to drive a potato into the rings. The inside circle scores 25 points; the next, 10 points; and the outside circle, 5 points.

Milk-bottle Bowling

Set three milk bottles on a line. The bottles should be 6 in. apart. Players try to roll a small ball between any two bottles without touching them. A successful roll scores ten points. Each player is allowed five balls.

BIG-TOP TABLE

Have this big-top cake as the centre of attraction on your party table. Arrange striped peppermint-stick tent poles round the edge. The tent

top is a circle of white kindergarten paper, about an inch larger in diameter than the cake. Cut four deep slits in the circle, equal distances apart, and overlap the adjoining edges so that the tent top will be peaked instead of flat.

Scallop the edge and bend down the part that overlaps the peppermint sticks. Colour this edge with red crayon and fasten the tent top to the mint sticks with egg white. Between the sticks place chocolate animals or miniature circus figures.

Arrange several clusters of balloons on the table and trail paper serpentines across it.

A mouth-organ clown makes an appropriate favour for a circus party. Cut the head from cardboard, and paste it to one end of the mouth-organ. Insert pipe-cleaner arms in the openings, just underneath the head.

Come and Get It!

Refreshments must include ginger pop and popcorn. You couldn't have a circus without these traditional palate-teasers. Complete the menu with party sandwiches, the big-top cake, and ice-cream clowns.

To make the clowns, place a cone at a rakish angle over a scoop of ice-cream. Decorate the peak with a red cherry button, and make the face of the clown with sections of glacé cherries or with raisins and cloves.

CAPTURE – THE – FLAG PARTY
23

FOR SCOUTS AND BOYS CLUBS

IN this game, resourceful, alert armies, employing all the tactical strategy of old and modern warfare, sometimes spend whole afternoons trying to ambush each other. So try it next time your club or scout troop gets together for a day of sport and adventure. You'll rank it "tops" for thrills and fun.

You will need plenty of space for this campaign of stalking, scouting, reconnoitring, and surprise attacks. An open field is the best place for it, but you can also play the game in the garden if it is large enough.

Organize your armies. Appoint two generals and prepare for action, for the war is about to begin.

THE BATTLE IS ON!

To describe the game, we'll call the armies the Reds and the Blues. The Reds' base of operations is on one side of a stone wall, brook, road, or stream. The Blues are located on the other side. The soldiers wear arm bands, bandanas, ties, or some other distinctive sign, so that they can quickly distinguish their friends from their enemies.

Each general has a flag on a 6-ft. pole. Within ten minutes after the battle signal has been given, the generals must hide their flags somewhere on their own battlefields, not more than 50 yds. from the boundary. The flag cannot be buried. It must be visible in all directions at fifteen paces—about 40 or 45 ft.—and can be supported only by the pole stuck in the ground. Guards are allowed to patrol the area near the flag, but may not stand closer than fifteen paces unless they spy the enemy approaching. Then they are allowed to close in.

Both armies have prisoner boxes inside their lines. The prison may be a tree stump or a square marked on the ground with stones or sticks. It must be within twenty yards of the border. Sentries may stand guard, but must remain 10 yds. away from the prison until a rescuer from the other side appears and attempts to free one of the prisoners. Then the sentry can try to tag the rescuer and put him in prison too.

When the flags are hidden, the battle begins. The object is to capture the enemy's flag. Players caught in enemy territory are put into prison. Team-mates try to elude the prison sentries and free their pals by touching them. If a rescuer eludes the guard and frees the prisoner, he and his team-mate are allowed to return to their own base. A player may set free only one prisoner at a time, however.

If the flag is captured, it must be carried across the boundary to the other side. That is when the battle rages, for if the person carrying the flag can be taken prisoner while he is still in enemy territory, the flag can be set up again. Carefully planned strategy is important. If team-mates work together, several can attempt to draw off the guards to give another member of their side a chance to sneak in and capture the flag.

Sometimes armies are so well matched that neither succeeds in capturing the other's flag. If that happens, and the war is still in progress at supper-time, award the victory to the team that has most prisoners.

Supper round the camp-fire, followed by a hearty sing-song, brings the party to a merry close.

24

Games for picnics and out of doors

Penny Hike

FORM two teams and choose two penny-tossers. The first group takes a left turn and starts walking. The second walks to the right. At the first street corner or crossroad, the penny-tossers in each group toss a coin to decide which direction to take. If the penny lands with the head showing, the group turns to the right. If it is "tails," the group turns to the left.

The two teams travel separately for half an hour, going wherever the penny dictates. It may take you in circles, or lead you on a long chase from home. But the penny's whims will make the walk a lively one.

Watch the time closely. After thirty minutes have elapsed, make a beeline for home. It is important to get back before the other team returns, for the losers have to stand the winners a treat.

Gipsy Patter-run

Go the way of the gipsies when you are planning your next hike or picnic. Following an old Romany custom, let four or five of the crowd start off for some unknown destination. Fifteen minutes later, the others try to pick up their trail. Their only clue to the direction of the gipsy band is a pile of stones, an arrow, or a handful of confetti at each fork in the road. According to tradition, gipsies marked their trails in this way to guide their wandering families who came after them.

By the time the boys and girls who are following the gipsy signs reach the place where the party is to be held, the band that started off first will have had time to unpack the food and prepare the meal.

Basket Picnic

Here is a way to inject a lively spirit into your next picnic. Each girl packs a picnic lunch for two—for herself and one of the boys. She does not know who is to share her meal, for the boys have to bargain for their food and for their luncheon companion.

Number the boxes and stack them in a pile. Choose one of the girls to be the banker. She gives each boy ten slips of paper of different colours, and assigns a different value to each colour. Red may be worth five points; blue, eight; yellow, ten. The banker is the only one who knows what the slips are worth.

After deciding for themselves which is the luckiest colour, the boys try to accumulate all the slips of that colour, by exchanging with the others. If, for example, a boy decides that yellow is worth most, he may be willing to trade two red slips for a yellow one.

After fifteen minutes of spirited trading, the banker announces the value of each colour. The number of slips a boy is holding determines his score. The one with the highest total gets box number one; the second, box number two; and so on.

Wouldn't the boys be surprised if they found identical lunches in all the boxes?

Firefly

This is a novel outdoor game for dark nights. If you are playing in the country, set boundaries so that the players will not wander too far away.

Choose three individuals to be the fireflies. They are given five minutes in which to hide. Each has a torch. Like the fireflies they are imitating, the hiders flash their lights on and off to lure the chasers. The other players then attempt to catch them.

As soon as a firefly has revealed his position with his light, he runs away. A fleet-footed runner can sometimes elude his captors for a long time and make the chase a breath-taking and exciting one. The players who capture the fireflies take their places after the three fireflies have been found.

Poison Bottles

Stand three "pop" bottles in the centre of the ring, some distance from each other. Players join hands in a circle, and by pulling and tugging try to make the others touch the bottles. Anyone who drops the hand of his neighbour, or knocks over or brushes one of the "poison" objects, is eliminated from the game.

Bottle-filling Race

Provide each player with a lemonade bottle with a short neck. Number the bottles and place them along a line. About 25 ft. away stand several buckets of water. There should be one for every four or five players.

Holding one hand behind his back and a paper cup in the other, a player runs to the bucket, fills his cup, runs back and pours the water into his bottle. The first one to get his bottle filled wins the game.

Balloon Swat

Give each player a paper swatter and tie an inflated balloon to the back of his belt. In this spirited contest, the players try to burst the other players' balloons while protecting their own.

Nose and Toe Tag

A player is free from being tagged by "It" only when he is holding his nose with one hand and touching his foot with the other.

25 More Indoor Games

Arches

TO piano or gramophone music, the players march round the room in a double circle. One pair of partners forms a bridge by raising their joined hands. The others march under the arch. From time to time the music stops unexpectedly, and the arch comes down. If anyone is caught inside, he and his partner leave the line of marchers and make another arch opposite the original one. Now there are two bridges to avoid when the music stops. Continue until all but two players have been eliminated from the marching circle.

Find your Partner and Stoop

Ask the children to take a good look at their partners, for they may have to find them in a crowd. Now make the players march in a double circle, the outside circle in one direction, the inside players in the other. When the players least expect it, blow a whistle. As soon as it sounds, the players rush pell-mell to find their partners, and stoop. The last couple down is eliminated from the game. Resume the marching and play until only one couple remains. They are the winners.

This game has action galore. Don't play it in the living-room unless the furniture has been removed.

Blow the Cone

Make a cone of stiff paper or cardboard. Pass a string through the cone, and attach each end to the back of a chair, keeping the string taut; or let two players hold the ends.

Place the cone near one end of the string. Give each player a turn at blowing into the wide end or fanning the cone with a piece of cardboard. Conduct a race between two teams or see which player can send the cone farthest with fewest puffs.

Buzz

The number "Seven" is buzz in this game. Players are seated in a circle. The first child starts the game by saying "One." The next says "Two." Each in turn adds the next number. But the player who is supposed to say "Seven," or any number which is a multiple of seven, or in which seven is mentioned, says "Buzz" instead. Thus the word Buzz is substituted for seven, seventeen, twenty-one, twenty-seven, twenty-eight.

Players who mistakenly call out a number when they should say "Buzz" are eliminated. The game requires quick counting and fast multiplying, but it is a "buzzing" good one.

Slogans (Advertisements)

Cut from magazines the slogans of well-known advertised products. Hold them up one at a time and let the players guess the product referred to. The first one to call out the correct answer scores a point.

Or cut out both slogans and pictures. Separate them, and give the same number of slogans and pictures to each of the players. The first to pair his set correctly wins the game.

Slipper Slap

Standing close together in a circle, the players pass round behind their backs a rolled newspaper or a stocking filled with cotton-wool. From time to time one of them swats "It," who is wheeling round in the centre trying to locate the swatter. If "It" is able to catch a player with the swatter in his hands, that person changes places with "It."

Hit the Clown

Hit the clown and win a prize. Draw the face of an open-mouthed clown on a large piece of cardboard. Cut away the mouth opening and stand the board on a chair or table.

Allow each player three turns to "toss the shot"—a dry sponge—through the clown's mouth.

Or, for a stunt that will really thrill the crowd, let one of your friends who is good at dodging make up as a clown, stick his head through an opening in a larger board and harangue the players to take a shot at him. Of course, he ducks as soon as they take aim. Anyone who can hit this fast-talking actor deserves a prize.

Dumb Spelling

Players take turns at spelling words chosen by the leader. But in this spelling bee the letters "T," "L," and "A" are unmentionable. Whenever they appear in a word, the player must indicate them by signs. Instead of saying "T," the player raises his right hand. For "L," he raises his left. When the letter "A" occurs in a word the player nods his head. For a lively head-nodding, hand-raising game, use such words as cattle, rattle, battle, bramble, thimble, dangle.

Hi There, Pat!

Two players kneel on the floor facing each other. Both are blindfolded and have boxing gloves on their hands. One is Pat; the other, Mike. Mike shouts, "Hi, there, Pat!" Pat answers, "Hi!" and ducks. The calling and answering continues as each boxer tries to find his opponent's position. Blows are delivered in that direction, but most of them fail to reach their objective. Each successful one scores a point.

Obstacle Race

With great fanfare, announce that you are going to award a handsome prize to the person who can, while blindfolded, walk over a row of obstacles without touching them. Before blindfolding the first player, arrange in a line a bottle, an egg, a plate, and a tub of water.

After the blindfold has been adjusted, remove the objects. If the floor is bare you can put down a few biscuits which will crunch like broken eggs when they are stepped on, and give your high-stepping friend some uneasy moments.

The joke is on the performer. He walks with measured steps. The audience helps with what he accepts as well-meant advice. Finally someone shouts, "You've done it," and he removes the blindfold only to discover that the floor was clear all the time. These "fooling" stunts should never be used on boys and girls who are timid, or easily embarrassed. Save them for the practical jokers in your crowd, the boys and girls who are always playing tricks on someone else.

Dry Whistle

Line up the players and give each a dry biscuit. After the starting signal has been given, the first one who can eat his biscuit and whistle a tune wins the game.

Mirror Vision

Two players form a team. One holds a quart jar on his head with his left hand. In his right he holds a tablespoon. His confederate holds a mirror in one hand and a dish of beans in the other. The boy with the jar on his head spoons the beans from the dish and by looking into the mirror tries to drop them into the jar.

Any number of teams may compete. The player who gets most in his jar at the end of five minutes wins the game.

Biscuit Swat

Two opponents lie prone on the floor facing each other. Fix a biscuit to each head, and arm each with a newspaper swatter. The players should be just so far apart that they can barely reach each other with their paper weapons. Holding one arm behind their backs, these "stretched-out" gladiators swat each other wildly in an attempt to break the other fellow's biscuit.

In this uproarious contest you can have two boys competing at a time, or form two lines with any number of competitors.

Hop, Skip, and Hope

Run this race in heats if necessary. Players hop across the room with inflated balloons between their knees. Their hope is that the balloons will remain whole until they reach the finishing line. If any burst, their owners are eliminated from the game.

High Jump

Four jumpers at a time vie with each other to get the first bite out of the doughnuts which are hanging from the ceiling, several inches above their heads. Competitors keep their hands behind their backs while they are jumping.

Ping-Pong or Feather Football

This game is played round a ping-pong or a large dining-room table. Play the match after supper if your table is already laid for refreshments.

Line up two teams as shown in the diagram. Players are not permitted to move from the spots where they are stationed. If a feather is used, players may not blow it unless they are holding on to the edge of the table with both hands.

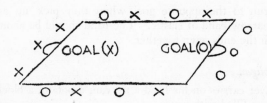

The ping-pong ball is fanned with a playing card. If any player touches the ball with his card, it constitutes a foul, and the opposing team has a free shot.

Put the feather or ball into play and score as in football.

Bean Dropping

One at a time, players kneel on a straight chair, lean over the back and drop fifteen beans into a milk bottle on the floor, just behind the chair. Easier said than done!

For other games consult the classified index.

RELAYS

In relay games, two or more teams compete against each other. Teams line up in parallel files behind a starting line. The first player in each team runs, walks, crawls, or performs whatever action is called for. Usually there is a line at the opposite end of the room or some kind of goal for each team. Indoors, players are frequently required to travel across the room, round a chair and back to the starting line. When chairs are used, they should be placed directly in front of each relay file so that all the teams have to travel the same distance.

As soon as the first player leaves the starting line, the second player moves up so that he will be in position and ready to start when the first player returns and touches his hand. After tagging the second player, the first one goes to the end of the line and the third one moves up in readiness for the second player's return.

All the teams are performing simultaneously and are racing each other to finish first. As soon as the last player on any team crosses the starting line on his return from the goal or opposite line, the game is won for his side.

A FEW RELAYS

Stretcher Race

Players run to the opposite goal, where they pick up and wriggle through a narrow band of elastic. The band should be about 18 in. in length, with the ends sewn together.

Happy Hooligan

Each player carries on his head a tin can, a potato, a block of wood, or a paper cup filled with water.

Bean Passing

Each player is given a paper cup and a drinking straw. Ten white beans are placed in the first player's cup. When the starting signal has been given, this player picks up the beans by inhaling them through his straw, and blows them into the second player's cup. The latter passes them, in the same way, to the third. The last player runs up and blows the beans into the first cup. The first team which returns the ten beans to the original receptacle wins the game.

This relay differs from the others. Lines are formed in the same way, but the players are not required to run to a goal.

HINTS ON QUANTITIES

YOU may find it helpful to consult this guide when you are planning menus for keen young appetites.

Milk . . . 1 quart gives 8 tea-cups.

Tea . . . ¼ lb. gives 50 cups.

Milk (for tea) . 1½ pints for 50 cups.

Coffee . . . ¼ lb. gives 25 tea-cups or 50 coffee-cups.

Sugar . . . ¾ lb. for 50 cups, allowing 2 lumps per cup.

Lemonade . . Allow 3 lemons to 1 quart.

Soup . . . 1 pint gives 4 soup cups.

Jellies and custards . 1 pint gives 6 individual moulds of average size.

Junkets . . . 1 pint gives 6 servings.

Ice cream . . 1 quart gives 12–15 scoops.

Sandwiches . . 1 loaf gives 30 slices. Allow one double slice, i.e. 4 small sandwiches, per head.

Small cakes, buns, sausage rolls, etc.—allow two per head.

FOR A PARTY OF TWENTY-FOUR GUESTS

Milk	3 quarts.
Milk (for tea)	1–1½ pints.
Tea (allowing 2 cups per head) . .	¼ lb.
Coffee	¼ lb.
Sugar	¾ lb.
Soup	3 quarts.
Jellies and custards . . .	4 pints.
Junkets	2 quarts.
Ice cream	2 quarts.
Sandwiches	2 loaves.
Small cakes, buns, etc. . . .	4 dozen of each.

Peach Melba

Place scoops of ice cream in glasses or fruit dishes. Place on top sugared peaches, cut into small slices. Add a dab of whipped cream and garnish with a glacé cherry.

Salted Almonds

½ lb. best almonds
2 tablespoonfuls olive oil
1 tablespoonful fine salt

Blanch the almonds and dry thoroughly. Put into a basin and pour oil over them. Mix thoroughly and let them soak for two hours. Stir occasionally so that the oil is evenly distributed. Put into a shallow baking-tin, sprinkle salt evenly over them, and bake in hot oven till they are light brown, turning now and then to ensure an even browning.

Apple and Orange Salad

Arrange crisp lettuce leaves on a glass dish. Cover with thin slices of apples and oranges. Sprinkle with grated cheese and finely chopped parsley. Serve with a thin salad cream.

Fruit Delight

Heat together 1½ cups of strained orange juice and one cup of lemon juice. Do not let the juices boil. Remove from stove and add one tablespoonful of gelatine which has been dissolved in a ¼-cup of water. Cool, and while it is cooling beat the mixture with an egg-whisk. When it thickens, add one cup of whipped cream. Serve in individual glasses, and decorate each with orange slices.

This can be made also by adding hot (not boiling) water to a packet of orange or other flavoured jelly, making the volume up to ¾ pint. Stir for a few moments, allow to cool but not to set. Then whisk to a foam. When thick, add whipped cream and serve as above.

Hot Spiced Lemonade

Add hot water and several bits of cinnamon bark to the lemon juice and sugar, and let it stand for five minutes. Stick four or five cloves into a slice of lemon and float in each drink.

Here are three dishes that you might like to try for the Valentine Party (Chapter 21) :

Funny-faced Pies

Line patty tins with thin pastry, and fill with minced meat or chicken. Cover with pastry crust from which small circles have been cut to represent eyes. Cut a curved slit below the eyes to give your funny faces grinning mouths. Bake in hot oven.

Bunny-rabbit Salad

Arrange halves of tinned pears, flat side downwards, on a large flat dish of shredded lettuce. Insert currants and small pink sweets for the eyes and noses and blanched almonds for the ears of the bunnies. Strips of marshmallows form the tails.

Chill until required, and serve with salad dressing.

Decorated Ice Cubes

Before filling the ice tray with water, place in each partition a glacé cherry or a small slice of lemon or orange. Add the water and freeze as usual in the refrigerator.

Float the cubes in the fruit punch bowl just before serving.

CLASSIFIED INDEX OF GAMES

GAMES FOR CHILDREN FROM 4–6 YEARS

Quiet Games

Alphabet Pictures	. . . 25	Of Whom am I Talking? . 36
Apples on a String	. . 43	Pinning Letters . . 24
Honey-Pots	. . . 26	Pussy wants a Corner . . 86
Of What am I Thinking?	.36, 53	

Active Games

A B C Hunt	. . . 24	Little Toy, what are you? . 49
Bubbles So High	. . . 62	Magic Circles . . . 62
Clock Hunt	. . . 66	Orange Toss . . . 77
Drop the Bell	. . . 49	Signal Man . . . 27
Hallowe'en Blind Man's Buff	. 43	Traffic Lights . . . 62
Jack, be Nimble	. . . 79	Whose is Biggest? . . . 62

Singing Games

Charlie over the Water	. . 79	Here we go round the Mulberry
Five Little Chickadees	. . 25	Bush (adapted) . . . 35

Races and Relays

Ankle Race	 78	Lollipop Race . . . 78
Balloon Push	. . . 78	Potato Race . . . 78
Broomstick Ride	. . . 79	Potato and Spoon Race . . 78

GAMES FOR CHILDREN FROM 6–10 YEARS

Quiet Games

Animal Guessing Game	. . 86	Ringer 141
Apples on a String	. . 43	Ring the Bell for Christmas . 108
Biddy, hold fast my Ring	. 87	Roll 'em In 142
Egg-box Toss	. . . 141	Santa Claus Artists . . 102
Engine Puzzles	. . . 31	Santa went to the grocer's . 49
Engine Toss	. . . 30	Simon Says . . . 85
Gift Maze	. . . 50	Telephone . . . 86
Hunt the Slipper	. . . 86	Tiddley Winks Goal . . 141
I Went to France	. . . 121	Traffic Lights . . . 62
Minister's Bunny	. . . 54	Treasure Trove . . . 50
O'Clock	. . . 87	Where was Bobby Standing? . 89
Of What am I Thinking?	.36, 53	Which Instrument is it? . . 86
Pinning Letters	. . . 24	Who has Tink's Tinkle Bell? . 68
Pussy wants a Corner	. . 86	Whose is Biggest? . . . 62

GAMES FOR CHILDREN FROM 6–10 YEARS—*contd.*

Active Games

A B C Hunt . . . 24
Apple Ducking . . . 96
Arches 149
Balloon Swat 148
Blow Out the Christmas Candles 107
Broken-down Engine . . 31
Cat and Mouse (also Peter and Hook) 65
Clap In, Clap Out . . 85, 107
Clock Hunt 66
Find Your Partner and Stoop . 149
Giant in the Ring . . . 43
Here I Brew 87
Hi There, Pat ! . . . 151
High Jump 153
Hill Dill 88

Hot Beans 85
King Has Toothache . . 123
Magic Circles . . . 62
Nose and Toe Tag . . . 148
Occupation 89
Pirates and Redskins . . 66
Red Rover 88
Run Into Your Cave . . 64
Sardines 94
Shadow Tag 66
Signal Man 27
Slipper Slap 150
Statues 88
Straddle Ball 50
Twelve O'Clock . . . 88
Walking the Plank . . . 65

Singing Games

A-Hunting We Will Go . . 84
Did You Ever See a Lassie ? . 84
Go Round and Round the Village 79
Here Come Three Dukes . . 82

Itiskit, Itaskit . . . 83
London Bridge . . . 81
Who has the Ring? . . . 54

Races and Relays

Ankle Race 78
Balloon Push 78
Broomstick Ride . . . 79
Flag Race 78
Happy Hooligan . . . 154

Hop, Skip, and Hope . . 153
Potato Race 78
Potato and Spoon Race . . 78
Stretcher Race . . . 154

GAMES FOR CHILDREN FROM 10–14 YEARS

Quiet Games

Actor Antics . . . 95, 111
Air Control 118
Air Objective . . . 118
Apple-paring Fortune . . 93
Bean Dropping . . . 153
Blarney Stammer . . . 131
Bubble, Bubble, Toil and Trouble 94

Buzz 150
Cahoots 100
Coffee Pot 100
Dry Whistle 152
Dumb Spelling . . . 151
Egg-box Toss . . . 141
Find the Leader . . . 128
Forfeits 131

GAMES FOR CHILDREN FROM 10-14 YEARS—*contd.*

Quiet Games—*contd.*

Get Rid of the Witch . .	94	Roll 'em In . . .	142
Ghosts	122	Santa Claus Artists .	102
Hunt the Slipper . .	86	Santa's Bag . . .	106
I Doubt It . . .	103	Secrets	130
I Went to France . .	121	Serial Story . . .	95
Illustrated Biographies .	113	Sir Valentine has lost his Hat .	127
In the Hat . . .	104	Slogans	150
My Grandmother Likes .	113	Telephone . . .	86
Name the Other . .	128	Tiddly Winks Goal . .	141
Odd or Even? . .	126	Treasure Trove . .	50
Pig	102	What Day Is Christmas ? .	106
Prophecies . . .	112	Wheel of Fortune . .	93
Ringer	141	Who Am I ? . . .	112
Ring the Bell for Christmas	108		

Active Games

Airborne . . .	121	Honeymoon Relay . .	129
Apple Bowls . . .	121	Indoor Golf . . .	122
Apple Ducking . .	96	King Has Toothache .	123
Arches	149	Lawyer, Lawyer . .	108
Balloon Swat . . .	148	Make a Date . . .	141
Basket Picnic . . .	147	Milk-bottle Bowling .	142
Biscuit Swat . . .	152	Mirror Vision . .	152
Blow Out the Christmas Candles	107	Nose and Toe Tag . .	148
Blow the Cone . .	150	Obstacle Race . .	152
Bombardment . .	119	Penny Hike . . .	146
Catch and Answer . .	129	Ping-Pong Hockey . .	121
Clap In, Clap Out . .	85, 107	Pirates and Redskins .	66
Deer Hunt . . .	123	Poison Bottles . .	148
Feather Football . .	153	Potato Golf . . .	142
Find Your Partner and Stoop .	149	Sardines . . .	94
Firefly	147	Similarities . . .	101
Gipsy Patter run . .	147	Slipper Slap . . .	150
Hi There, Pat ! . .	151	Straddle Ball . . .	50
High Jump . . .	153	Walking the Plank . .	65
Hit the Clown . .	151	Witches' Clatter . .	94

Races and Relays

Bean Passing . . .	154	Hop, Skip, and Hope .	153
Bottle-filling Race . .	148	Mirror Vision . .	152
Flag Race . . .	78	Potato and Spoon Race .	78
Happy Hooligan . .	154	Stretcher Race . .	154
Honeymoon Relay . .	129